CORNWALL
FOR EVER!

KERNOW
BYS VYKEN!

A good sword and a trusty hand
    A merry heart and true,
King James's men shall understand
    What Cornish lads can do.

And have they fixed the where and when?
    And shall Trelawny die?
Here's twenty thousand Cornish men
    Will know the reason why!

Robert Stephen Hawker
Trelawny

**HRH The Prince of Wales, Duke of Cornwall
with Princes William and Harry.**

To understand ourselves we need to know where we have come from and to know something of our roots. This excellent book will help you to do this and I hope will encourage you to discover more about the wonderful place that is your home – Cornwall.

I am enormously proud and privileged to be the Duke of Cornwall and I have always believed that Cornwall and the people who live here are very special. This is so because of the place that Cornwall is. It is an ancient land, formed of ancient rocks, shaped by the sea, the wind, the rain and the sun. It has an incomparable coastline, magnificent uplands, secret valleys and tranquil estuaries. Its villages and towns, its harbours and ports, each have their own Cornish distinctiveness.

The uniqueness of Cornwall lies also in its history. Its very many prehistoric sites, its medieval buildings and its latter-day monuments all add to Cornwall's distinctiveness. These, too, have helped shape the Cornish people, with their own special beliefs, myths and folk stories, their language and dialect, their courage, their sense of adventure and their inventiveness. The Cornish have always made their mark on the world, at home and abroad, on the sea, down the mines and on the land. I believe we can all take pride in Cornwall's heroes and heroines, as well as in the ordinary people of Cornwall who often had to endure conditions of great adversity. They are examples to us as we begin our journey in a new Century and a new Millennium.

But we cannot take Cornwall's future for granted. If Cornwall is to be successful in times to come, and if Cornwall and its people are to keep their Cornishness, it will need all the optimism, confidence, determination and skill that you – our next generation – can muster. You will all come to carry an important responsibility for preserving the Cornish way of looking at life, the Cornish language and dialect, the Cornish culture and identity, and the very appearance of Cornwall.

I pray that the picture of Cornwall you will find in this book will reinforce your love of this particularly special part of Britain.

introduction

Cornwall is
a VERY special
place

Whether born here or recently arrived, everyone takes great pride in calling Cornwall 'home'. Many thousands of us, dressed in the famous Cornish colours of black-and-gold, have followed the fortunes of the Cornish rugby team to Twickenham. Others have celebrated St Piran's Day, 5th March, some by walking across the dunes at Perranporth to visit St Piran's ancient Celtic cross or to imagine him arriving on the beach from Ireland some fifteen hundred years ago.

here's twenty thousand Cornish

Still others want to learn about Cornwall's own language, so similar to Breton and to Welsh, if not to speak it fluently then at least to understand it a little or to name our homes in Cornish. Many delight to feel the fresh air in their faces as they hike across the wide expanses of Cornwall's moors or walk the coastal footpath that takes them to hidden coves or lofty headlands on the lengthy journey from Marsland Mouth to the Tamar estuary. Some of us are lucky enough to live on the Isles of Scilly but many more are drawn across from the mainland to experience the sub-tropical luxuriance of the islands that are perhaps the Lyonnesse of the King Arthur legend.

men will know the reason why.

There is much to grip the imagination and stir the heart in Cornwall. Our distinctive landscape is strewn with remains of former times, from Bronze Age standing stones and stone circles to the gaunt engine houses and crumbling stacks of the more recent mining era. Contrasts are dramatic, from the high, bare cliffs of North Cornwall to the silent, tree-cosseted creeks of the south coast estuaries. Tourists flock to Looe, Polperro, Bude, Newquay and St Ives but even in high summer there are quiet nooks and deserted lanes where tranquillity may be found. Blue, clear skies with an almost Mediterranean light are threatened suddenly with brooding storm clouds away to the south west. Calm, silvery seas give way to an angry swell and crashing surf.

Men an tol

Artists, novelists and poets have been enticed to Cornwall by this exciting environment. Stanhope Forbes established the Newlyn School of painting at the turn of the twentieth century. Daphne du Maurier lived in and wrote about Cornwall for almost her entire adult life. The late Poet Laureate, Sir John Betjeman, lover of Cornish churches and Cornish railways, spent much time at Trebetherick on the north coast. But Cornwall has produced its own fair share of painters and writers, from the famous abstract painter Peter Lanyon to equally well known novelists and poets of international stature such as D.M. Thomas, Jack Clemo and Charles Causley. Today there are many young people who celebrate Cornwall in song and verse, or in dance and other art forms. Some form Cornish rock bands, others create Cornish web-sites.

***Sunblast* by Sir Terry Frost, one of the many artists working in Cornwall.**

Throughout history, Cornish people have been just as creative. In medieval times (the period from about 1000-1500), wonderful plays such as the *Ordinalia* and *Beunans Meriasek* (the Life of St Meriasek) were written in the Cornish language and performed all across Cornwall in out-door theatres.

In the Industrial Revolution, Cornwall led the world in deep mining and steam engineering. Cornwall was at the cutting edge of technology, and Cornish scientists and inventors were world leaders.

Richard Trevithick invented the steam locomotive and he also took Cornish expertise to new lands, helping to develop mining in South America in the early nineteenth century. Others followed in his footsteps, and soon Cornish emigrants – the Cousin Jacks and Cousin Jennies – were to be found across the globe. The Cornish mined for silver in Mexico and Peru. They opened the copper and lead mines of South Australia and the United States, and they played an important role in the Gold Rushes to California, Australia, New Zealand and South Africa.

Back in Cornwall, this new industrial society warmed to the religious teachings of John Wesley, and soon Wesleyan and other Methodist chapels sprang up from the Tamar to Land's End. These Methodists wrote Cornish carols, organised tea-treats, held services in Gwennap Pit, and joined brass and silver bands. Some tried to stamp out Cornish wrestling but others became champion wrestlers.

During the Industrial Revolution Cornwall led the world in technology. Richard Trevithick was one of many who put Cornwall firmly on the map. Illustrated here is his famous locomotive which successfully pulled 20 tons of iron and up to seventy passengers at Pen-y-darren in South Wales in February 1804.

But Cornwall is not just about the past; it is about the present and the future. Although Cornwall has suffered more than enough from the changes in mining, farming and fishing, there is at the turn of the twenty-first century a mood of optimism and self-confidence which insists that Cornwall remains capable of great things. 'Hi-tech' industries have taken root here, evidence that in the computer age geographical location is hardly relevant to economic performance. Many people have recognised that Cornwall's special qualities are great strengths, to be cherished and built upon as Cornwall seeks to find its way in the new Britain, in the new Europe and on the international stage. Visions for the future will vary, but each demands that Cornwall's children should have the opportunity to live, learn and work here.

In this book, produced to mark the Millennium and given to every young person aged eighteen and under in education in Cornwall, the story and spirit of this very special place are presented in word and picture.

Cornwall Timeline

This timeline marks key events in Cornwall's history.

400,000–10,000BC

PALAEOLITHIC

(EARLY STONE AGE)

Little evidence of human activity in Cornwall during this period.

10,000–4,000BC

MESOLITHIC

(MIDDLE STONE AGE)

'Hunter-gatherers' settle around the coastline and on the uplands.

4,000–2,400BC

NEOLITHIC

(NEW STONE AGE)

2,400–600BC

BRONZE AGE

600BC–AD50

IRON AGE

Time of great social and economic development, including the spread of farming and increased monument construction. Fortified settlements, such as Carn Brea, appear.

Introduction of metalworking, especially bronze, using Cornwall's natural resources of tin and copper. Construction of monuments such as standing stones and stone circles.

Iron replaced bronze for weapons and tools. The Celtic language (forerunner of modern Cornish) appears in Cornwall. People live within defended 'rounds'. Forts built on hill-tops and headlands for trading, manufacturing and military purposes.

AD43–AD410

**ROMAN OCCUPATION
OF BRITAIN**

577

600

Romans arrive in Britain
but make little impact in
Cornwall. Cornwall
becomes a 'pagus' or
district of the south
western province of
Dumnonia. Departure of
Romans leaves eastern
Britain open to Anglo-
Saxon settlement.

Battle of Deorham
Down, near present-day
Bristol. Anglo-Saxon
victory leaves the West
Welsh (Cornish)
separated from the
Welsh of Wales.

St Piran's oratory
founded at Perranporth.
The 'Age of Saints'.

936

1066

1280-1290

Anglo-Saxon King Athelstan fixes the east bank of the River Tamar as the border between Cornwall and Wessex. Cornish are evicted from Exeter.

Norman Conquest. Robert de Mortain becomes Earl of Cornwall and builds castle at Launceston.

Mappa Mundi (Map of the World) in Hereford Cathedral shows the four constituent parts of Britain as England, Scotland, Wales and Cornwall.

1307

1337

1497

Tinners' Charter
granted by Edward I.
The Stannaries provide
Cornwall with legal
and political semi-
independence.

Edward the Black Prince,
eldest son of Edward III,
becomes first Duke
of Cornwall.

Cornish Rebellion.
Michael Joseph 'An Gof'
and Thomas Flamank lead
the Cornish army to
defeat at the Battle of
Blackheath (London).

1508

1549

1595

'Charter of Pardon' granted by Henry VII restores the Cornish Stannary Parliament.

Cornish 'Prayer Book Rebellion' opposes new Protestant Prayer Book and its use of the English language.

Spanish raiders attack Mousehole, Newlyn, Penzance and Paul.

1642-6

1688

1689

**Civil Wars, in which the
Cornish Army fights for
the Royalist cause.**

**Bishop Trelawny
imprisoned in the Tower
but later released.
Acquitted of 'sedition'.**

**Packet ships set up first
international mail
service.**

1743

1777

1801

John Wesley's first of forty visits to Cornwall.

Death of Dolly Pentreath. She is often described as the 'last' speaker of the Cornish language, but there is evidence that other speakers may have survived into the 19th century.

Richard Trevithick's road locomotive trialled in Camborne. The hey-day of Cornish mining and engineering.

1807

1815

1840

Miners' safety lamp
is invented by
Humphry Davy.

End of Napoleonic Wars.
Start of Cornwall's 'Great
Emigration'.

Hungry Forties' in
Cornwall, leading to food
riots and continuing
emigration.

1846

1859

1866

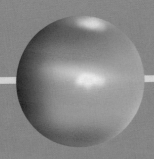

John Couch Adams discovers the planet Neptune.

Royal Albert Bridge at Saltash connects the Cornish railway system to the rest of Britain.

The 'crash' of Cornish copper mining. Many mines are closed and many people emigrate.

1880

1903

1904

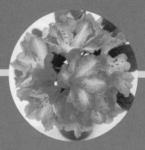

**Foundation stone of
Truro Cathedral laid by
HRH The Duke of
Cornwall.**

**The rhododendron
arrives in Britain at
Caerhays Castle.**

**Henry Jenner writes his
*Handbook of the Cornish
Language* and secures
Cornwall's membership
of the Celtic Congress.**

**The Great Western
Railway introduces its
Cornish Riviera Limited
train and opens the way
for the development of
mass tourism.**

1914-1918

1928

1931

**The First World War.
Thousands of Cornish
people are killed in the
fighting.**

**First Cornish Gorsedd
(Gorseth Kernow), held at
Boscawen-un.**

**Donald Healey from
Perranporth wins the
Monte Carlo Rally.**

**Healey continued to
race, develop and build
his own sports cars,
which in the 1950's
became the famous
Austin Healey.**

1939-1945

1961

1997

Second World War. Many Cornish men and women are killed or wounded.

Tamar Road Bridge opened.

Celebrations in Cornwall to mark 500th anniversary of the events of 1497.

1998

1999

2000

Closure of South Crofty, Cornwall's last tin mine.

Cornwall defeats Gloucestershire at Twickenham in the Rugby Union County Championship.

Cornwall awarded Objective One status

Total eclipse of the Sun on the morning of 11th August.

Dawn of the new Millennium.

Bob Berry

landscape

'The LIFE of a region depends ultimately on its GEOLOGIC substratum, for this sets up a chain-reaction which passes, determining their character, in turn through its streams and wells, its vegetation and the animal life that feeds on this, and finally through the type of human being attracted to live there.

In a profound sense also the structure of its rocks gives rise to the psychic life of the land... these unhewn slabs of granite hold the secret of the country's INNER LIFE'

ITHELL COLQUHOUN
THE LIVING STONES OF CORNWALL
1957

The Cornish landscape has been shaped by weather, nature and human activity. Many millions of years ago, Cornwall was given its geological shape and form, and has been weathering ever since. Nature has fitted into this landscape, establishing a flora and fauna (plants and animals) which have found harmony in the environment. Humans at first adapted themselves to this landscape but later began to adapt it to their own needs and desires. Today there is little or no wholly natural landscape in Cornwall, almost all of it having felt the hand of humankind.

Clodgy Point
near St Ives, west Cornwall.

The Cornish coastline has evolved over many thousands of years.

Twelve thousand years ago the Ice Age was ending, and seas were beginning to rise, engulfing land that had been exposed for millennia. The coastline of Cornwall extended then some five miles beyond its current limit, while the Isles of Scilly were part of the mainland and Britain was joined to continental Europe. As these northern lands became warmer, so humans arrived, so-called 'hunter-gatherers' searching for food in the newly developing hunting grounds. In Cornwall, the first evidence of these people is found in and on the ground – small, level platforms on which they may have built their shelters, together with stone and flint tools.

A prehistoric axe-head, displayed in the Royal Cornwall Museum in Truro.

Bob Berry

The seas rose slowly until, some six thousand years ago, the Channel was formed, cutting Cornwall and Britain off from the continent. Increasingly tied to the land, people in Cornwall began to grow crops and to erect monuments, including the impressive quoits (or portal dolmens) which may have been of religious or political significance. They demanded considerable skill and co-operation on the part of those who built them, suggesting the emergence of tribal territories as well as a desire by these people to leave their marks upon the landscape.

In modern times, excavation and the study of surface features have revealed the remains of the rectangular stone or wooden houses in which these early people lived – the first evidence of permanent or semi-permanent dwellings in Cornwall. Although we do not know the size of families or how these houses were roofed, we have in the settlements upon Carn Brea clear evidence of both trade and warfare, a clue to how society was developing in those far off times.

**Trevethy Quoit,
near St Cleer.**

Of course, much of the evidence from long ago has been ploughed out, or built over, or even swallowed by the ever-encroaching sea, but the well-preserved remains to be found on upland areas such as West Penwith, the Lizard and Bodmin

Moor are a good indication of how these early people lived. The landscape around Rough Tor, for example, is a vivid testament to their activity, with its hundreds of stone houses and hedge banks, while that near Minions is an astonishing array of round houses, circles, standing stones, burial cairns, and field systems.

About four thousand years ago, some people in Cornwall – probably the leaders, or elite – were beginning to use copper, tin, bronze, gold and silver for tools and jewellery. Some of these metals were found locally but there is also evidence for trade in such artifacts with Ireland and Brittany, establishing commercial and cultural links that would endure for millennia.

All the while, the temperature had been rising, so that people in Cornwall would have lived in a climate very much like that of southern France today. However, by about 1000BC the climate had started to cool, becoming rather like that of modern Cornwall – perhaps even colder and wetter. This deterioration in climate caused the development of damp, peaty ground on the uplands, encouraging people to leave the moorlands and to establish themselves on the lower ground.

An example of gold Lunulae, or moon shaped jewellery, which can be found in the Royal Cornwall Museum in Truro.

Chun Castle, in the far west of Cornwall. Note the track leading from the entrance of the fort to the even older Chun Quoit (see bottom left of picture)

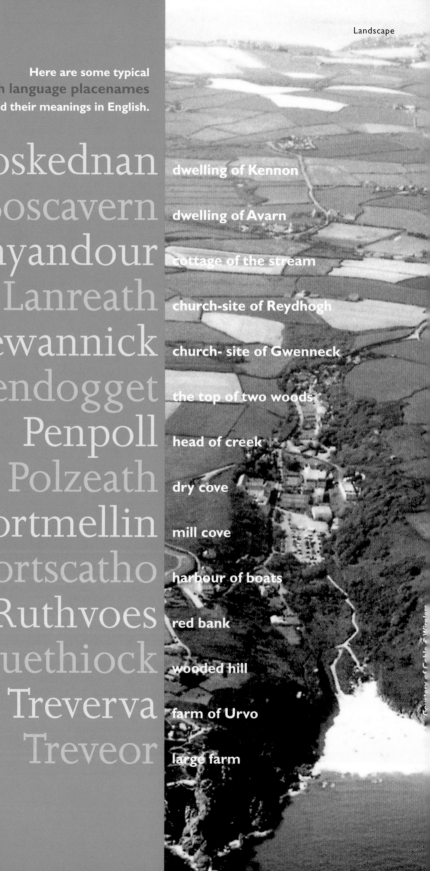

Here are some typical **Cornish language placenames** and their meanings in **English**.

Boskednan	dwelling of Kennon
Boscavern	dwelling of Avarn
Chyandour	cottage of the stream
Lanreath	church-site of Reydhogh
Lewannick	church-site of Gwenneck
Pendogget	the top of two woods
Penpoll	head of creek
Polzeath	dry cove
Portmellin	mill cove
Portscatho	harbour of boats
Ruthvoes	red bank
Quethiock	wooded hill
Treverva	farm of Urvo
Treveor	large farm

Treryn Dinas, also known as Treryn Castle, near Porthcurno.

By 800BC hill forts and cliff castles had begun to appear in the Cornish landscape, and by 600BC a new metal, iron, was being used for domestic artifacts, tools and weapons. At much the same time, farming centres had become enclosed; so-called 'rounds' in which the main farm buildings were surrounded by an earthen bank and ditch. Small, high-walled fields, known today as 'Celtic fields' (they are are still to be found in parts of Cornwall) had also appeared by this time. The Roman occupation had almost no effect upon this landscape. By the post-Roman era, Cornwall was developing as a land of hamlets, of open undefended groups of farmsteads, often with a name beginning with the prefix 'Tre-': Cornish for a farming estate or settlement.

Celtic fields near **Morvah, west Cornwall.**

Traditional Cornish stooks are still part of the harvesting landscape of Cornwall.

Graeme Norways

Zennor
in west Cornwall.

The Anglo-Saxon settlement of southern Britain also left Cornwall relatively untouched. English placenames in the far north-east of Cornwall and between the Lynher and Tamar rivers may be evidence of cultural contact with Anglo-Saxon newcomers rather than the displacement of indigenous people by invaders. Certainly, most Cornish people remained Cornish-speaking and continued to live in their scattered hamlets – there were no large villages. The familiar Cornish rural landscape, with its pattern of farmlands, of trackways, of fords and bridges, was by now taking shape.

Bedruthan Steps
in north Cornwall.

The National Trust

The Domesday Book survey of 1086, compiled after the Norman conquest, reveals that by that time there were many well-established estates in Cornwall. William I gave many of these to his half-brother, Robert de Mortain, who built the impressive castle at Launceston as a powerful symbol of Anglo-Norman rule in Cornwall. Other castles appeared and new churches were built but farming patterns were by now well entrenched, the rural landscape changing little during the Norman period. As the weather improved, some of the upland areas were reoccupied for farming, while secondary incomes were made from tin streaming and cloth manufacture. The highest ground remained common grazing land, as it was until as recently as 300 years ago, identified by the Cornish word 'goon' (or 'woon'), the equivalent of the English 'down'.

In the fourteenth and fifteenth centuries, plague – the 'Black Death' – swept through Cornwall. As the population dwindled, many of the lowland farms became vacant, and were re-occupied by farmers abandoning the poorer upland areas. But the medieval period also saw an increase in trade, encouraged in part by the Duchy of Cornwall which controlled large estates and other resources, particularly in mid – and east Cornwall. Shipping, shipbuilding and victualling became increasingly important aspects of the Cornish economy, as did the growing practice of tin streaming. Foweymore (modern Bodmin Moor) and Blackmore (above St Austell) became major tin streaming centres, and the sometimes huge scars of this activity can still be found on the Cornish landscape today.

Launceston Castle
built by Robert de Mortain,
William I's half brother.

Early mining
depicted in illustrations
from *De Re Metallica*
published in 1550.

Cornish hedge
at Tintagel Church.

Indeed, close observation of Cornwall today will allow a peep into this medieval landscape, not least the familiar 'churchtown' with its solid, stone church with fifteenth-century tower, surrounded by a cluster of houses and farm (or at least the remains of one) coming right up to the churchyard wall. But by the end of the sixteenth century, the Cornish landscape was changing quickly. Open fields were being enclosed behind high 'Cornish hedges', and farming hamlets were consolidated into single farms as family and social structures changed. Change was accelerated from the middle of the eighteenth century, as Cornwall began to industrialise and as the extractive industries grew in size and importance. The landscape of large tracts of Cornwall was transformed as mining for copper and tin, and for other metals such as lead, silver and iron, came to dominate the Cornish economy.

By the middle of the nineteenth century, the mining districts of Cornwall were defined by the wild, treeless wildernesses that had been created, dramatic landscapes littered with the paraphernalia of deep mining (engine houses, machinery, shaft openings) and marked with huge burrows or mine dumps. Cornwall's reputation at the time as a barren 'West Barbary' rested as much on the bleakness of its mining districts as it did upon the ruggedness of its moors and cliffs.

1898

Germoe in 1898
and below as it
looks today.

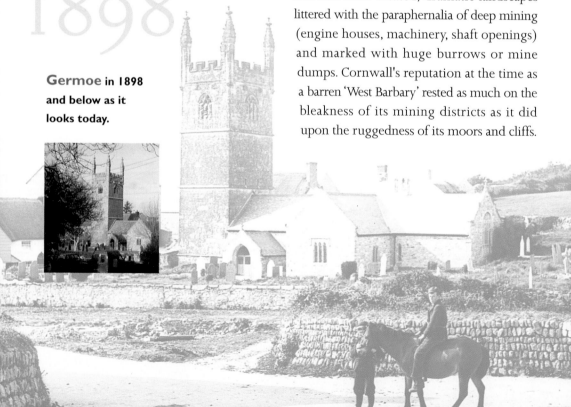

With the wholesale abandonment of the Cornish mines from the 1860s onwards, an eerie emptiness and silence descended on many of these mining landscapes, an atmosphere that can still be felt today.

Engine houses perched on the cliffs at Botallack, just north of St Just-in-Penwith.

Granite and slate quarrying also had an effect on the Cornish landscape, the former in areas such as St Breward and Cheesewring on Bodmin Moor, or around Mabe and Constantine, the latter in most spectacular fashion in the ancient quarry at Delabole. China clay quarrying has also had a dramatic impact, especially in the so-called 'china clay country' north of St Austell where the lives of villages such as Treviscoe, Trewoon, St Dennis, St Stephen-in-Brannel, Bugle, Stenalees, and Foxhole have been shaped by the dominating environment of clay. Today, the once characteristic 'white pyramids' are being replaced by huge grassed-over mounds, the broken landscape of places such as Carloggas Downs giving way to smooth swathes of green, but the clay country remains a distinctive Cornish environment.

The China Clay Country. Gorse and other moorland foliage gradually encroaches on the white pyramids, the pools remain a milky, turquoise blue-green.

Mike Newman

The Engine House,
an enduring image of
Cornwall.

The significant impact of industrialisation on the Cornish landscape was mirrored in a similar impact on the built environment, with tramways, chapels, mine buildings, harbours, and rows of miners' cottages springing up across Cornwall. Although this industrial hey-day has passed long since, much of this survives, and the ruinous, ivy-clad engine house is now a familiar image of the Cornish landscape.

The decline of mining was matched by changes in the farming economy. The number of agricultural workers declined as demand for manual labour fell, and many small farms were amalgamated. Since 1945, Cornish hedges have disappeared at an alarming rate as field sizes were increased to cope with new mechanisation, altering the appearance of the landscape as well as destroying important wildlife habitats. In some cases the removal of hedges has led to serious erosion problems, and today there is greater sensitivity towards the Cornish hedge, even to the extent of new hedges appearing up and down Cornwall alongside new housing or industrial developments.

Remains of mine workings
at Kenidjack Valley,
near St Just-in-Penwith.

The growth of mass tourism has also had an effect on the Cornish landscape, with caravan sites large and small dotted across the countryside, and themes parks carving out large spaces for themselves. Huge car-parks have appeared, roads have been widened, and 'redundant' fishermen's or farm

Graeme Norways

Bob Berry

labourers' cottages have been done-up as second homes. Industrial estates or 'business parks' have also appeared on the landscape, sometimes constructed on so-called 'green field' sites (countryside) and at others on reclaimed 'derelict land' such as old mining sites.

Elsewhere, 'derelict land' has been cleared up with the aid of government grants. Open shafts have been capped, ruined buildings consolidated, toxic waste treated, rubble cleared away, dumps levelled and covered with grass. Some critics complain that this process 'sanitises' the landscape and makes it less 'Cornish'.

It would be wrong, however, to imagine that the Cornish landscape we see today is just the result of the industrial period, of mining, quarrying, tourism and other activities. Much of Cornwall remains deeply rural, with high open country but also densely wooded valleys, creating habitats for animals which range from badgers and foxes to perhaps even the mythical 'Beast of Bodmin Moor'.

Bluebell Wood

Welcomed by environmentalists as an appropriate use of alternative technology, Cornish wind farms are criticised by some as intrusive and noisy.

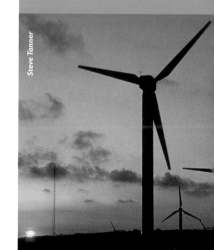

Steve Tanner

the built environment

'The Cornish...
...were boat-builders,
craftsmen and engineers,
rather than architects. For
this reason the buildings
of Cornwall are mostly
homely and not at
all grand'

JOHN BETJEMAN
CORNWALL: A SHELL GUIDE
1964

The ultra-modern satellite communication
dishes at Goonhilly Downs, viewed across
the mysterious expanse of Croft Pascoe Pool –
said to be haunted on dark and foggy nights by
a phantom lugger.

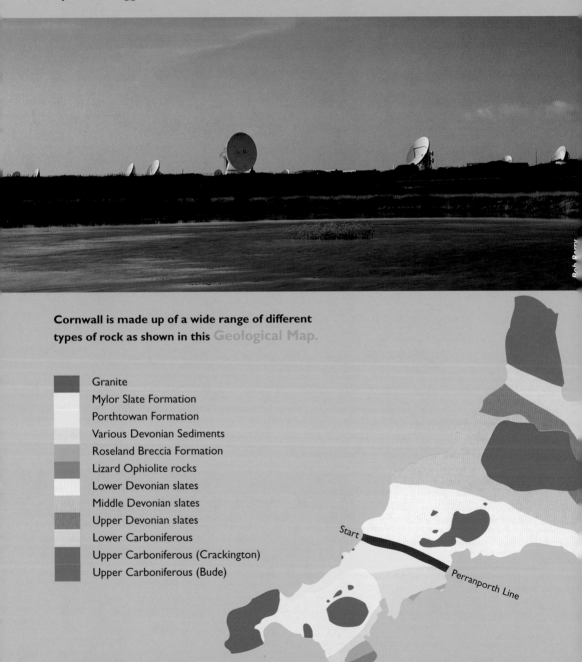

Cornwall is made up of a wide range of different
types of rock as shown in this Geological Map.

Granite
Mylor Slate Formation
Porthtowan Formation
Various Devonian Sediments
Roseland Breccia Formation
Lizard Ophiolite rocks
Lower Devonian slates
Middle Devonian slates
Upper Devonian slates
Lower Carboniferous
Upper Carboniferous (Crackington)
Upper Carboniferous (Bude)

Start

Perranporth Line

The term 'built environment' makes us think of houses and schools, factories and hospitals, shops and supermarkets, but in fact it has a much broader meaning, including just about everything that humankind has thought to construct in the landscape. In Cornwall, there is much that is distinctive in this 'built environment', from the stone circles of Bronze Age times through to the engine houses of the nineteenth century and on to today's wind farms. Our maritime situation has given us lighthouses and harbours; railways and roads have brought viaducts and bridges. Modern technology has delivered the satellite dishes of Goonhilly and Morwenstow.

Alex Scheele

The geology of Cornwall, with its granite and slate, has profoundly influenced the built environment. In earliest times, moorstone – the great hunks of granite that litter upland Cornwall – was used by prehistoric peoples to erect the standing stones, round house remains and burial chambers that we can still find from the Scillies to the Tamar. Dotted across Cornwall are the curious 'quoits' (or 'portal dolmens' as they are sometimes known to archaeologists), such as Lanyon Quoit near Madron or Trethevy Quoit near St Cleer, which once may have been burial tombs or had perhaps other religious or territorial significance.

Lanyon Quoit, near Madron, one of Cornwall's famous 'portal dolmens'. The old theory that such quoits are the remains of ancient burial tombs has been replaced recently by new ideas. Some archaeologists think the quoits may have been religious monuments. Others argue that they were territorial markers, showing the area ruled by a particular tribe or group of people.

Ballowall Barrow, near St Just-in-Penwith, a complex entrance grave or 'chamber tomb' as it is sometimes known.

In west Cornwall and on the Isles of Scilly, there are numerous so-called 'entrance graves', such as the spectacular Ballowall Barrow near St Just-in-Penwith or the beautifully preserved Bant's Carn on St Mary's. On St Mary's and elsewhere in the Scilly Isles, these graves stand in the midst of ancient field systems, evidence of the close links between life and death in those far-off prehistoric days.

Scattered across Cornwall are the mysterious stone circles such as the Merry Maidens, near Boleigh on the coast road between Penzance and Land's End, and the Hurlers near Minions on Bodmin Moor. Our prehistoric ancestors may have erected these circles for religious reasons, but in the eighteenth and nineteenth centuries new legends emerged to account for their curious construction.

The Rumps, near St Minver, one of the finest 'cliff castles' in Cornwall.

The Merry Maidens were said to be naughty girls turned to stone for daring to dance on a Sunday, while the Hurlers were thought to be young men similarly punished for playing the Cornish game of hurling on the Sabbath.

Chun Castle, on the heights of West Penwith, is an early example of a Cornish hillfort. During the so-called Iron Age period many more of these impressive fortifications were built — ranging from Caer Bran in the far west to Castle-an-Dinas near St Columb Major, Castle Dore near Fowey, Castle Canyke at Bodmin, and the awe-inspiring Warbstow Bury on the River Ottery in North Cornwall. Dating from the same period are the so-called 'cliff castles' built on headlands around the Cornish coast. Trevelgue, near Newquay, and Rame Head in south-east Cornwall, are good examples but perhaps the best-known 'cliff castles' are the Dodman, near Gorran Haven, and the Rumps, near St Minver.

The Hurlers near Minions on Bodmin Moor. This is an archaeologically rich part of Cornwall, where evidence of prehistoric peoples is found side by side with the remains of the more recent copper and tin mining industries.

Carn Euny, in Penwith, is a courtyard house settlement. Like many ancient sites in Cornwall, it is open to the public.

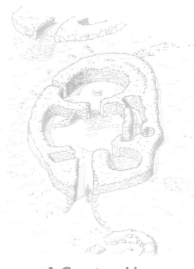

A Courtyard house settlement shown above as it looks today and as it would have appeared in Iron Age or Roman times. Below a shaft of light finds its way through a crack to illuminate the underground fogou at Carn Euny.

Some of these hillforts and cliff castles may have been occupied (although not always continuously) for centuries. Some may have been inhabited from Iron Age times in the fourth century BC, through the period of Roman occupation (from about AD55 until the departure of the Legions from Britain in AD410 or thereabouts) and afterwards, as Roman authority collapsed and as Cornwall was faced later with the emerging power of the Anglo-Saxon kingdom of Wessex.

There is little physical evidence of the Roman occupation in Cornwall (a few milestones, a small military fort at Nanstallon, near Bodmin, the remains of a villa at Magor, near Illogan, Roman pottery found at Carvossa, near Probus) but dating from the Iron Age and Roman periods are the so-called courtyard house settlements, the best preserved of which today are Chysauster and Carn Euny. Both are to be found in Penwith. These, together with the sixty or so other sites known to exist elsewhere in Cornwall, consist of interlocking houses. At Carn Euny there is also a fogou (the Cornish word for 'cave'), an underground chamber which was possibly a cold storage for food but may have served as a hideout or perhaps have been used in pre-Christian religious ceremonies.

Illustrations by Craig Weatherhill.

Norman church doorways at Manaccan
and St Germans, **the latter showing the**
characteristic zig-zag or chevron design.

The holy well at Dupath,
near Callington.

The arrival of Christianity in Cornwall in the sixth century
led to new constructions in the countryside. From saint's
oratories, Celtic crosses and well-chapels to the first churches,
Christian architecture became increasingly significant in the
Cornish landscape. The churches that we find across Cornwall
today often incorporate early features (including ancient
Celtic crosses in their churchyards), with elements of Norman
architecture (such as the zig-zags or chevrons above the
church doors at Morwenstow, Kilkhampton and St Germans)
and much from the medieval period and beyond.

Constantine Church,
near Falmouth, has a
magnificent example of a
'three-stage' tower.

Characteristic of so many Cornish
churches is the three-stage fifteenth-
century tower, such as those at Week St
Mary, St Cleer, Lanlivery and Constantine.
Despite the hardness of the granite, the
skill of the Cornish craftsman is evident
in the intricate carving at St Mary
Magdelene, Launceston, or on the tower at
Probus church.

St Mawes Castle and Pendennis Castle (below) were built at the mouth of the River Fal, by Henry VIII.

Restormel Castle, **close to Lostwithiel, is an example of a circular castle commonly known as a 'shell keep'.**

The ruins of Tintagel Castle, **depicted in an engraving by Samuel Buck in 1734.**

The Norman invasion in the eleventh century also brought a new style of military architecture to Cornwall, the medieval castle. At first simple 'motte and bailey' structures with wooden stockades, these castles were soon rebuilt in stone. A magnificent example is Launceston castle, today still dominating the River Tamar and the gateway to Cornwall as it has done since medieval times. At Tintagel there is a ruinous but still striking castle perched on the cliff's edge, associated in legend with the mythical King Arthur and the site perhaps of Cornish royal power long before the Normans thought to build their fortification there. At Trematon, near Saltash, and Restormel, near Lostwithiel, are fine examples of so-called 'shell keeps' or circular castles, the latter the twelfth-century fortress of the Black Prince. Crowning St Michael's Mount are the castle and house that grew out of an earlier monastery, and at Pendennis and St Mawes are two rather more 'modern' castles – fortresses that were built by Henry VIII in the sixteenth century to counter the threat of Spanish attacks.

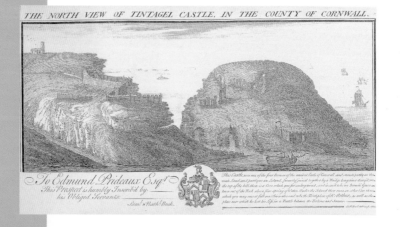

Paul Watts

Paul Watts

Other Cornish buildings of note that have survived from the medieval period include the remains of the so-called 'Duchy Palace', at Lostwithiel, and Cotehele House – set above the Tamar near Calstock and today preserved lovingly by the National Trust. The National Trust has also preserved the wonderful Old Post Office at Tintagel, and has been in the forefront of saving and restoring many other important Cornish buildings. Trerice, near Newquay, is a superb example of a Tudor gentleman's house (and a former residence of the notable Arundell family), and at Lanhydrock in East Cornwall is the extensive house and estate of the Robartes family. Although gutted by fire in the nineteenth century, Lanhydrock was carefully rebuilt in its original seventeenth-century style. Near Torpoint, on the site of the earlier dwelling of Richard Carew, author of the celebrated History of Cornwall of 1602, is Antony House, another National Trust property, built in the eighteenth century in the beautiful buff-coloured Pentewan stone.

Of course, not all of Cornwall's fine houses are owned by the National Trust, and amongst notable examples in private hands are Trewithen, near Probus (also built of Pentewan stone), Place (the seat of the Treffry family at Fowey), the mysterious Godolphin near Helston, and Caerhays Castle near Gorran Haven – not really a castle at all but a great house built in the nineteenth century, famous today for its magnificent Cornish gardens.

Five famous Cornish Houses: (from top)
The Old Post Office, **Tintagel;**
Trerice, **near Newquay;** Antony,
near Torpoint; Lanhydrock, **near**
Bodmin; Godolphin, **near Helston.**

It was in the nineteenth century that much of the 'built environment' of Cornwall that we recognise today was erected. Ancient borough towns such as Saltash, Helston, Camelford, Mitchell, Penryn and Grampound, not to mention Truro, had inherited significant architectural features from earlier times, but it was in the late eighteenth and nineteenth centuries that 'urban' Cornwall really began to take shape. The miners' terraces and cottages in the mining districts around Camborne, Redruth, St Austell, Callington, St Day, St Just-in-Penwith and elsewhere are as important a part of the Cornish heritage as the grand houses described earlier, and so too are the many industrial remains from that period. In the Tamar Valley, on Caradon Hill, on United Downs, along the Great Flat Lode behind Carn Brea, dotted around Wendron and Marazion, on the cliffs at Botallack, and at countless other locations are the engine houses and stacks of Cornwall's copper and tin mines.

Cotehele, built above the Tamar, near Calstock, is a National Trust property.

Miners' cottages near St Day.

The Duchy Palace at Lostwithiel can still be seen today, though sadly only a fragment remains of what was an extensive building.

Cornish World

'CORNISH LADS ARE FISHERMEN, AND CORNISH LADS ARE MINERS TOO, BUT WHEN THE FISH AND TIN ARE GONE WHAT ARE THE CORNISH BOYS TO D'

The headframe at South Crofty is a silent but powerful remembrance of Cornwall's proud mining history.

The Treffry Viaduct, situated deep in the lush Luxulyan Valley of mid Cornwall.

A Great Western Railway train crosses over Brunel's Royal Albert Bridge, built in 1859, and enters Cornwall at Saltash.

In Camborne, the headframe at South Crofty is a poignant memorial to the survival of tin mining until very recent times, while the white 'lunar landscape' around St Austell tells us that china clay production remains an important part of the Cornish economy. The crumbling remains of the Perran Foundry, near Perranarworthal, soon to be restored as a heritage tourism attraction, are also testament to Cornwall's great industrial period, as is the incredible Treffry Viaduct in the Luxulyan Valley (today in the ownership of the Cornwall Heritage Trust) – a superb monument to Cornish engineering skills, a structure which was both acqueduct and a mineral tramway viaduct. Remains of other mineral tramways and indeed later railway lines (including the entire North Cornwall network, closed in the 1960s) are also to be found, and here and there are still the 'stumps' of Isambard Kingdom Brunel's wooden viaducts that once carried the main-line through Cornwall.

Brunel's Royal Albert Bridge across the Tamar at Saltash remains very much in use, as is the main-line railway that snakes its way down to Penzance.

Just as Cornwall's medieval churches are a distinctive part of the built environment, so too are the many Methodist chapels that appeared from the Tamar to Land's End in the late eighteenth and nineteenth centuries. Sometimes grand buildings set amidst growing industrial towns such as St Austell or Camborne, at others more modest buildings set deep in the Cornish countryside, these chapels reflected the enthusiasm of the competing Wesleyan, Bible Christian, Primitive Methodist and other denominations. Many were designed and built by local Methodist activists, ordinary people with skills as carpenters or stonemasons, but some of the more ambitious structures were the work of well-known professional architects. Silvanus Trevail, for example, built the imposing chapel that still stands by the roadside at Edgcumbe between Helston and Penryn, together with the chapel at Mount Charles (St Austell) that was pulled down in the 1990s.

Trevail also designed a number of other important buildings in Cornwall, such as the 'King Arthur's Castle Hotel' at Tintagel and a great many of the village schools that are still in use today. Another important designer, from earlier in the nineteenth century, was Goldsworthy Gurney (born near Padstow) who, amongst his many inventions (including the system of flashing lights for lighthouses), built Bude Castle on a concrete raft base to demonstrate that this method of construction was sound. Today, the concrete raft is a familiar part of building construction in Cornwall and elsewhere.

Paul Watts

Camborne Centenary Chapel, **a fine example of a large Methodist chapel.**

Cornwall Record Office

King Arthur's Castle Hotel, **still in use as a hotel today, was designed by the famous Cornish architect Silvanus Trevail.**

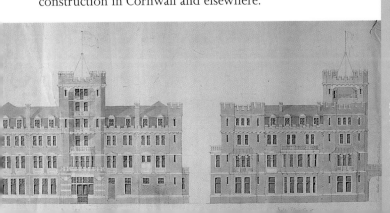

Cornwall Record Office

John Passmore Edwards, born at Blackwater, near Truro, in 1823, was a newspaper owner – not an architect or builder, let alone an inventor. However, he was so successful that he wanted to use the vast wealth that he had created to help other people, and to that end he had built a splendid array of libraries, hospitals and other public buildings – quite literally from Liskeard to Newlyn – which even today are a distinctive part of the Cornish built environment.

Passmore Edwards funded many public buildings across Cornwall, including Newlyn Art Gallery near Penzance, and many libraries such as Redruth Library. The latter currently houses the Cornish Studies Library, an unparalleled collection of books, newspapers and other published material relating to Cornwall.

The building of Truro cathedral was the high point of nineteenth-century building in Cornwall, for although construction did continue after 1900, notably in the erection of fine hotels in places such as Bude, Newquay and Falmouth, the building industry as a whole was hit by Cornwall's economic downturn. Between the First and Second World Wars there were relatively few additions to Cornwall's housing stock, so that after 1945 there was a severe housing shortage. One answer was the production of 'Cornish Units' by the china clay industry; bungalows, houses and other dwellings made out of prefabricated concrete components. Very successful within Cornwall, Cornish Units were also used extensively in other parts of Britain to make good War losses.

A sturdy bungalow built in the 'Cornish Unit' style during the 1950s.

A scene of great activity in 1886 as Cornwall's new cathedral in Truro, begins to take shape.

Courtesy of Truro Cathedral

The bold architecture of the Tate Gallery St Ives, with a Barbara Hepworth sculpture fittingly displayed.

Bob Berry

By the late 1960s, as people began to move to Cornwall in ever greater numbers, so there was an ever increasing demand for new houses. To respond to this demand, new housing estates sprung up across Cornwall. Although many dwellings, with their white or pebble-dashed exteriors, represented a new kind of popular 'Cornish vernacular' architecture, not everyone thought that they fitted in with the existing built environment. By the 1990s, therefore, there was greater emphasis on using traditional designs and materials wherever possible. One aspect of this was the happy practice of building new Cornish hedges around new housing or industrial estates and along new roads, instead of the brick walls or fencing found 'up-country'. More controversially, Cornwall also saw the erection of a number of startlingly ultra-modern buildings, such as the Law Courts in Truro, the Tate Gallery at St Ives, and the huge Biomes emerging at the Eden Project.

But for all this recent activity, the built environment of Cornwall remains distinctive, for the most part an agreeable balance of the 'Old' and the 'New', settling well into the broader Cornish landscape of which it is a part.

Construction work well under way at the Eden Project near St Austell.

Photographs: The Eden Project

the sea

With granite ribs and black basaltic brows
And flanks of dark and metal-bearing slate,
All veined and patined o'er with snowy quartz,
Cornubia rises storm-swept from the sea,
A land of legend and strange mystery,
Of tragic frown and sun-kissed ecstasy.
He who would know the depths of that old heart
For aeons cradled on the changeless rock,
For aeons guarded by the encircling sea,
Must seek the silence of the purple moors,
Must know the fury of her mighty surf,
Must mark the splendours of her sea-born clouds.

A.G. FOLLIOTT-STOKES
THE CORNISH COAST AND MOORS
1912

Legend has it that a man named Trevelyan was the only person to escape the drowning of Lyonnesse, having madly galloped to safety just ahead of the rushing sea. This legendary event is remembered to this day in the white horse incorporated in the coat of arms of the Vyvyan family, into which the Trevelyans married.

After storms tree trunks and roots have been exposed on the beach at Mount's Bay, evidence of a now submerged forest that once may have stretched to St Michael's Mount and beyond – perhaps to the mythical Lyonesse. The photograph dates from 1883.

In Cornwall you are never far away from the sea. Surrounded on three sides by the ocean and on the fourth almost cut off by the Tamar, Cornwall is virtually an island. This maritime environment has played a major role in moulding the character of Cornwall and its people, and is a key element in our history.

Much of Cornwall's folklore, for example, has to do with the sea. The story of the 'lost land' of Lyonnesse tells of a place that once lay beyond Cornwall, a country of towns and churches and farms which one day was suddenly inundated by a huge tidal wave that swept all before it. Richard Carew in his *Survey of Cornwall* of 1602 said that fishermen off the coast of Cornwall sometimes dredged up ancient window frames and other relics of the 'lost land', while other legends insist that Lyonnesse was once the home and perhaps the final resting place of King Arthur.

Often legends have more than a glimmer of truth, a vague collective memory of something that happened a very long time ago. The story of Lyonnesse, perhaps, tells us that once the Isles of Scilly were joined to the Cornish mainland, and that over many centuries they were gradually inundated by the encroaching sea to give us the archipelago – St Mary's, St Agnes, Tresco, Bryher, Samson, St Martin's and the other islands – that we recognise today.

Gibson

An aerial view of the Isles of Scilly. The Scillies formed one land mass until perhaps as late as the eleventh century.

The inundation of the islands in relatively recent historical times may help to explain why the 'lost land' of Lyonnesse is such a strong theme in Cornish folklore.

Frank Gibson

Godrevy Light, the
source of Virginia Woolf's
inspiration.

Bob Berry

Sometimes legends tell us about the powerful fears and hopes that people have experienced in times past. As well as being a 'harvest field', as the Cornish called it, full of marine life to sustain local communities, the sea also had a dark and violent side. When sailors and fishermen were lost in great storms at sea, this was seen by our distant ancestors as the work of the sea-god who demanded perpetual sacrifice. This belief, perhaps, explains the eerie folktale, recorded by Robert Hunt in the mid-nineteenth century, of an incident late one night on Porthtowan beach. A strange voice was heard calling three times from the sea, 'The hour is come but not the man'. Suddenly a figure all in black appeared on the hill-top, pausing briefly before rushing headlong into the waves and disappearing for ever.

Similar fears may be responsible for the many Cornish mermaid stories, while a more recent legend – celebrated every year at Mousehole as Tom Bawcock's Eve (23 December) – tells how Tom Bawcock's boat braved the angry storm to bring home a bumper catch of fish to save his village from starvation.

The sea has also featured strongly in books about Cornwall. Robert Louis Stevenson's *Treasure Island*, with characters such as 'Squire Trelawney' and 'old Redruth', is thought to have been set partly in Cornwall. So too is *Five Go Down to the Sea*, one of the series of Famous Five stories by the children's novelist, Enid Blyton. Many of Daphne du Maurier's Cornish novels also have a strong maritime aspect. *Frenchman's Creek*, for example, is a story of piracy and romance set on one of the silent, wooded creeks of the Helford River. Virginia Woolf's *To the Lighthouse* was inspired by Godrevy, near St Ives, although in her novel she transferred the location to the Western Isles of Scotland.

Mike Newman

'The hour is come but not the man'.

Helford River is the setting for **Daphne du Maurier's** *Frenchman's Creek.*

The National Trust

Hawker's Hut at **Morwenstow, carefully preserved by the National Trust.**

A Newlyn School painting, Harvesters of the Sea, by Ralph Todd (1856-1932). Many more of these fine works can be seen at the Penlee House Gallery and Museum in Penzance.

The sea has also proved an important inspiration for other writers. Robert Stephen Hawker, vicar of Morwenstow in the mid-nineteenth century, composed many of his poems and ballads while looking out to sea from the little hut made of driftwood on the cliffs near his church. 'Hawker's Hut', as it is known, is still there and lies close to the Cornish coastal path at Morwenstow.

For artists, too, the sea has been significant, both for inspiration and as a subject for paintings. At the end of the nineteenth century, Stanhope Forbes and the Newlyn School of painters captured in their work the lives of ordinary fishing folk at Mousehole, Newlyn and Penzance. On the other side of the Penwith peninsula, at St Ives, a more abstract school of painters emerged, but one that still owed its inspiration to the ever-present sea. Alfred Wallis was an artist of special note, his 'primitive' paintings of boats and harbours appealing to children and adults alike.

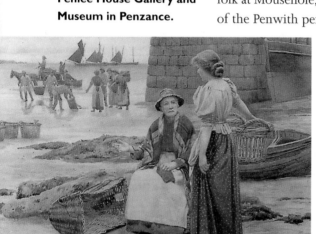

One of Alfred Wallis' delightful 'primitive' paintings The Wreck of The Alba. It can be seen today at the Tate Gallery in St Ives.

e ever present sea ... y p...
ornwall's economic life. Although wrecking and
nuggling are often portrayed in books as romantic
tivities, they were in fact a hard and often dangerous
ay for people to make a living. Although there is no
cord of the Cornish deliberately luring unsuspecting
ips on to the rocks, there is plenty of evidence to show
at local people habitually plundered vessels that had
een wrecked on Cornwall's dangerous coastline. The
orth coast was especially treacherous, giving rise to the
rim rhyme:

From Padstow Point to Lundy Light

s a watery grave by day or night'

hen the Good Samaritan was wrecked on Bedruthan Steps in October
346, at the height of the Hungry Forties when many people in
ornwall were on the verge of starvation, the locals thought the wreck
blessing and stripped the vessel bare:

St Keverne in 1898 from
the **SS Mohegan, one**
of the many ships lost
on the Cornish coast.

THE GOOD SAMARITAN CAME ON SHORE

O FEED THE HUNGRY AND CLOTHE THE POOR

BARRELS OF BEEF AND BALES OF LINEN

NO POOR MAN SHALL WANT FOR A SHILLIN'.'

John Oates

Genteel wreckers!
Women and children sift
through the wool cast
ashore from the cargo of
a ship wrecked on the
Cornish coast about 1900.

1923

The five-masted schooner **Adolf Vinnen** was wrecked off the Lizard in a gale in February 1923 during her maiden voyage from Germany to Barry in South Wales. Her entire crew of twenty-four sailors was rescued, using the rocket-line apparatus shown above. Although only a few years after the First World War, the Cornish coastguards risked their lives to save the German seamen.

Of course, the Cornish also acquired a reputation for heroism risking their own lives to pluck drowning men and women from the raging seas. Henry Trengrouse, from Helston invented the rocket-line, for many years the standard device used by coastguards to get a life-saving line aboard a stricken ship. All around the Cornish coast, lifeboats have been stationed at strategic points, and even today the Cornish lifeboats are amongst the busiest in the British Isles. In a terrible tragedy in 1981 the Penlee lifeboat was lost with all hands when it ventured out one dark December night to answer the call of a foundering ship.

A Cornish lifeboat at **Cadgwith** in the early 1920s. Today the boats, men and women of the Royal National Lifeboat Institution are on call and often in action 365 days a year around the Cornish coast.

www.photo-point.co.uk

On December 19th 1981 the crew of the **Penlee Lifeboat** went to the aid of the stricken ship *Union Star*. Despite their valiant efforts, all eight lifeboatmen lost their lives. A helicopter pilot who witnessed the rescue attempt said '*they were truly the bravest eight men I've ever seen who were also totally dedicated to upholding the highest standards of the RNLI*'.

1981

www.photo-point.co.uk

In the eighteenth and early nineteenth centuries, great risks were also taken by Cornish smugglers as they slipped across to Brittany or the Channel Islands to collect their illegal cargoes. Cawsand Bay in south-east Cornwall and Mount's Bay in the west were especially notorious for their smuggling activities. At Prussia Cove 'Captain' John Carter (who lived from 1749 to 1809) was known as the 'King of Prussia', such was his reputation as a bold and successful smuggler.

By the middle of the nineteenth century, smuggling as an everyday activity had almost disappeared; the Preventive men employed by the government to stop this illegal trade by then were too well organised and powerful. Many smugglers turned their hands to more honest trades, especially fishing. The pilchard fishery, though it had declined by the end of the nineteenth century, was of great importance to communities such as Cawsand, Mevagissey, Newlyn and St Ives.

The Sea

Paul Watts

The Huer's Hut at Newquay. The huer would scan the sea, crying 'Hevva' to alert the fishing fleet if a shoal of pilchards was sighted.

HEVVA! HEVVA!

At Newquay an old 'huer's hut' survives, from where the huer or watchman once scanned the sea to spot the pilchard shoals coming in close to shore. 'Hevva! Hevva!', the huer would cry, alerting his colleagues who would then put to sea immediately to catch the fish. In those days the pilchards were the fishermen's 'best friends', the streets and alleyways of fishing villages awash with pilchard waste as the fish were prepared for export to their principal market, the Catholic countries of southern Europe. As an old Cornish rhyme put it:

Pilchards have been packed in the traditional way since the 1500s. They can still be seen today at The Pilchard Works Museum in Newlyn.

**'Long life to the Pope,
Death to our best friends,
And may the streets
run in blood'.**

Tate Gallery

Tucking a School of Pilchards. This painting by Charles Napier Hemy, and the remarkably similar photograph below, convey all the excitement and energy of a pilchard haul off the Cornish coast in the nineteenth century.

Despite the decline of the pilchards, both inshore and deep-sea fishing survived, and today Newlyn has still one of the most important fishing fleets in the United Kingdom. Mevagissey, Looe, Padstow and other Cornish ports also sport their own fleets, while many individual fishermen still operate from small coves in pursuit of crabs, lobsters and other species. There are still important oysterbeds on the Helford and the Fal.

Luggers from Newlyn, fishing in Mounts Bay in the early nineteenth century.

In the early nineteenth century, as Cornwall's industries developed and as mining and steam engineering came to dominate the Cornish economy, so the sea became important in the service of the new industries. Coal was imported from South Wales and copper ore was exported for smelting at Swansea. Timber for mining props was brought in from Norway, and from ports such as Hayle huge Cornish beam engines and other mining machinery were sent overseas to destinations as distant as Mexico and South Australia.

Canals were built at Bude and at Looe, and the River Tamar became an important industrial waterway as sailing barges plied up and down from the copper mines around Callington, Calstock, Gunnislake and Morwellham. New ports and quays such as Portreath, Devoran, Par, Pentewan, Charlestown, Trevaunance and Bude were established to deal with the new industrial trade, while others were re-fitted to meet the demands of the changing economy. The expansion of china clay in the nineteenth and twentieth centuries meant increased activity for ports such as Par, Fowey, Charlestown and even Looe. Others became centres of shipbuilding and ship repair, an industry that survives today in places such as Falmouth and Penzance.

Cornwall had also been important for centuries as a home of the Royal Navy and of the Packet service. The Falmouth Packets, which ran from 1688 until 1850, carried the Post Office's mail for far-flung destinations in the Mediterranean, the Caribbean, and North and South America. The Navy also helped in the growth of Falmouth as a maritime centre, where in the eighteenth century Admiral Edward Boscawen ran what was almost a private Cornish Navy (or so his critics said), and Torpoint was always a Naval town.

Admiral Edward Boscawen, Lord Falmouth of Tregothnan, known affectionately as 'Wry-necked Dick' as a result of a nasty wound received in a naval battle. Another nickname was 'Old Dreadnought', taken from the name of one of his ships, a reflection of his fearless exploits such as the capture of the famous French ship *Temeraire* off Lagos in 1759. When it was rumoured that Boscawen had fallen out with the government of the day, one of his supporters wrote: *'No! that cannot, shall not be; it would put the very ocean in a storm and the large continent of Cornwall into a rebellion'.*

National Portrait Gallery

Sea-King 'Search and
Rescue' helicopter from
RNAS Culdrose.
As well as rescuing
countless people from
incidents all around the
Cornish coast, the 'SAR'
helicopters (as they are
known) operate far into
the North Atlantic to
save those in peril on
the sea.

Today, the Royal Navy maintains a strong presence
in Cornwall, with its vast training establishment
HMS RALEIGH at Torpoint and the Royal Naval
Air Station (HMS SEAHAWK) at Culdrose, near
Helston, the largest helicopter base in Europe.

Tourism, of course, has also had a major impact on
Cornwall. It was Cornwall's dramatic seascape and
coastline that first attracted many tourists to Cornwall,
and in the late nineteenth and early twentieth centuries the
Great Western Railway promoted what it saw as the almost
Mediterranean qualities of the 'Cornish Riviera'. Penzance,
Falmouth, St Ives, Perranporth, Newquay, Fowey and Looe
were all developed as important seaside resorts served by the
Great Western. The Southern Railway, not to be left out,
developed its North Cornwall routes to Padstow and Bude as
'King Arthur Country', helping to popularise destinations
such as Boscastle and Tintagel.

Mike Newman

Fishing survives in Cornwall, despite the depletion of fish stocks and the consequent resrictions on the amount of fish allowed to be landed.

www.photo-point.co.uk

The surf life-saving tradition of Cornwall is as proud as those of Australia and America.

Energy and exertion, muscle and movement, are brought alive in this shot of a highly competitive Cornish gig race.

The sea remains an important leisure resource today but not only for tourists. Many local people are involved in water activities of one sort or another. Cornish gig-racing is especially popular, and all around the coast but especially from Sennen to Bude many Cornish people are involved in the 'surfing scene', an important sub-culture which has become an increasingly visible part of the Cornish identity.

Cornwall has also hosted the Celtic Water Sports Championships, a reminder for us that it was the sea that first allowed the growth of contacts between Cornwall and its Celtic neighbours, especially Brittany. For Cornwall, the sea has always been a window to a wider world of trade and friendship with other peoples.

Mike Newman

Mike Newman

Not Malibu or Bondi, but Fistral, showing that Cornish surfing can be at least as exhilarating and as challenging as that of California or Australia.

www.photo-point.co.uk

Robyn Davies, the champion female surfer from Cornwall, in action.

people

'Much has been written and
said lately about the boys
and girls of Cornwall
not knowing a lot
of the history or
people of our
County.'

Edith Martin
Do You Know Cornwall?
1936

Here are a few
words of Cornish:

Chy - House

Bal - Mine

Scath - Boat

Den - Man

Benen - Woman

Flogh - Child

Mam - Mother

Tas - Father

Cath - Cat

Ky - Dog

Porth - Harbour

Mor - Sea

Forth - Road

Bre - Hill

Cornwall has been inhabited since prehistoric times. We know about the earliest people from their archaeological remains, evidence that has been found in the excavation of sites such as burial chambers or the foundations of houses. But we are unsure about how and when people arrived in Cornwall from elsewhere in Britain or continental Europe. The first 'hunter-gatherers' probably arrived at the end of the Ice Age twelve thousand years ago, when the climate was improving and Britain was still joined to the continent.

Later peoples came by boat but the old idea that there were successive mass invasions, in which earlier peoples were killed or driven out by newcomers speaking new languages and using new technologies, is increasingly questioned by experts. Instead, historians now think that these 'invasions' involved relatively few people who, because of their military or economic strength and superior technologies, were able to impose their ways upon existing populations. The use of iron for tools and weapons, from about 600BC, represented an important technological change, and its adoption in Cornwall seems to have coincided with the spread of the Celtic language, the forerunner of modern Cornish.

Illustration by Katy Oliver, BA (Hons) Illustration, Falmouth College of Arts

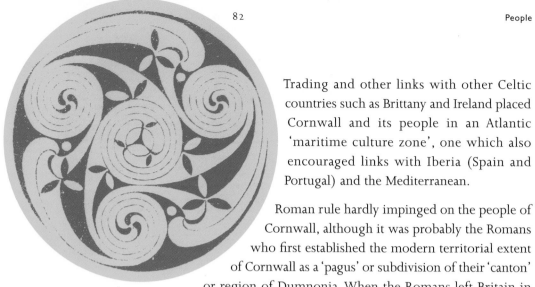

Distinctive Celtic designs are found in each of the Celtic countries in ancient times and are still popular today.

Today the 'maritime culture zone' of Western Europe is known as the 'Atlantic Arc', a group of countries and regions which at the beginning of the twenty-first century still have a lot in common.

Trading and other links with other Celtic countries such as Brittany and Ireland placed Cornwall and its people in an Atlantic 'maritime culture zone', one which also encouraged links with Iberia (Spain and Portugal) and the Mediterranean.

Roman rule hardly impinged on the people of Cornwall, although it was probably the Romans who first established the modern territorial extent of Cornwall as a 'pagus' or subdivision of their 'canton' or region of Dumnonia. When the Romans left Britain in about AD410, these islands were threatened with Anglo-Saxon intruders, who came first as raiders and later as settlers. Although it is now thought that there were relatively few of these invaders, their impact was immense, leading to the spread of the English language and to the establishment of Anglo-Saxon kingdoms which later became England. Although the eastern fringe of Dumnonia (modern Devon and western Somerset) eventually fell to the Anglo-Saxon kingdom of Wessex, Cornwall itself remained intact, its culture and language continuing to be Celtic. For reasons that are still not clearly understood, there was at this time a substantial movement of people from Cornwall to Brittany, reinforcing the links between the two territories.

It was also about this time that the legends of King Arthur first appeared. We do not know if Arthur ever existed, and some people think that he is actually several historical figures rolled into one, a semi-legendary hero who has absorbed the exploits of various Celtic warrior chieftains who fought against the Anglo-Saxons in various parts of Britain. This may explain why the Arthur legend is strong in Somerset, Wales, Brittany, northern England and southern Scotland, as well as in Cornwall, but for many people King Arthur remains an essentially Cornish figure – with 'his' castle on the cliffs at Tintagel.

Illustration by Christina Brine, BA (Hons) Illustration, Falmouth College of Arts

King Doniert's Stone, near St Cleer. Doniert is said to have drowned at Golitha Falls in the nearby River Fowey in AD875 or thereabouts.

Documentary evidence, written down on parchment or even carved in stone, began to appear during the years after the Romans' departure, and from various sources we learn of the existence of shadowy Cornish kings and chieftains such as Teudar (who features in the later Cornish miracle play *Beunans Meriasek*), Dumgarth (probably the Doniert commemorated on a stone near St Cleer), Mark (a central figure in the Tristan and Iseult story), Geraint (said to have been killed by the English at the battle of Llongborth, perhaps present-day Langport in Somerset), and Hywel – reputed to have been the last independent king of Cornwall.

After the Norman conquest in 1066 we begin to learn more about people in Cornwall. Often, however, these are figures from outside, such as Robert de Mortain, William I's Breton half-brother who was given a substantial land grant here, and the Black Prince, son of Edward III and the first Duke of Cornwall, who fought against the French in the great victories of Crécy in 1346 and Poitiers in 1354. There were, however, Cornish people who made a significant impact 'up-country', such as John Trevisa, born about 1340 (possibly at St Mellion or St Enoder), who was an Oxford scholar and went on to become chaplain of Berkeley Castle in Gloucestershire. Another was Tamsin Bonaventure, born at Week St Mary in 1450, who became Lady Mayoress of London in 1497. The last of Tamsin's three wealthy husbands was the London merchant, Sir John Percival, who had been made Lord Mayor in 1497, and she used the riches accumulated from her successful marriages to found a school in her native village in Cornwall.

1497 was also a year of Cornish rebellion. The rebel leaders, Michael Joseph 'An Gof' ('the Smith') of St Keverne and Thomas Flamank of Bodmin, are today well known. More obscure are the lesser gentry and farmers who supported the rebel cause, men like Richard Borlase of St Wenn and William Ham of Stoke Climsland, or those such as Nicholas Enys of Luxulyan and John Pendyne of Pendeen who were later fined for their parts in the rebellion. In 1548, on the eve of the Cornish 'Prayer Book Rebellion' of 1549, William Kilter, yeoman of Constantine, and Martin Geoffrey, priest of St Keverne, were amongst those executed as traitors, and after the rebellion itself there were a great many hangings up and down Cornwall. Richard Bennett (vicar of both St Veep and St Neot) was executed, as were Simon Morton (vicar of Poundstock) and William Alsa (vicar of Gulval).

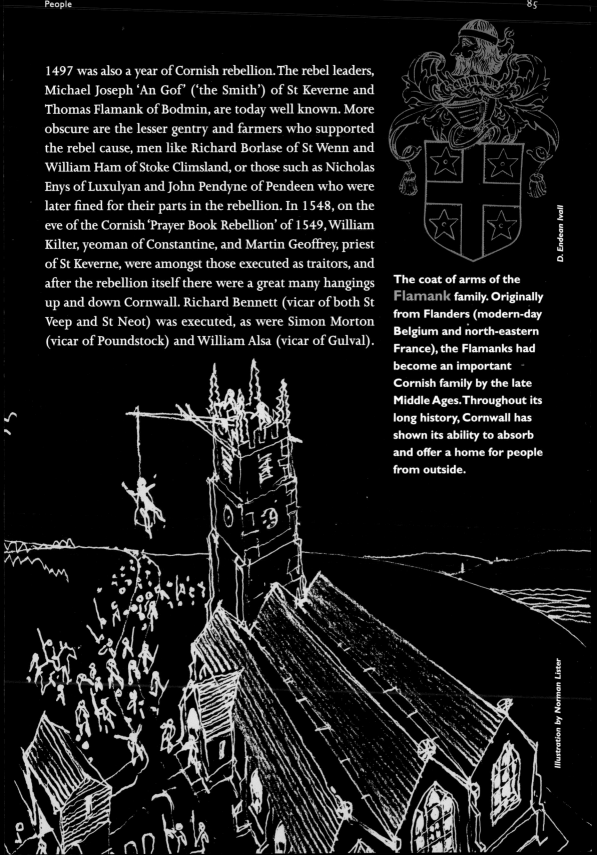

D. Endean Ivall

The coat of arms of the Flamank family. Originally from Flanders (modern-day Belgium and north-eastern France), the Flamanks had become an important Cornish family by the late Middle Ages. Throughout its long history, Cornwall has shown its ability to absorb and offer a home for people from outside.

Illustration by Norman Lister

Sir Bevil (or Beville) Grenville, Cornish hero of the Civil Wars celebrated in 'The Gate-song of Stowe' by Robert Stephen Hawker:

After 1549, many Cornish people became Protestant but some clung to the Catholic faith and were persecuted for their beliefs. Notable amongst these were Francis Tregian of Golden, near Probus, and Cuthbert Mayne, his priest. In 1577 they were both arrested and sent for trial at Launceston, where Mayne was subsequently executed. For those who had become Protestant, the wars with Catholic Spain gave them an opportunity to fight for their religion. Others, the pirates and privateers of Cornwall, including the Killigrew family of Arwenack (Falmouth), used the wars to make money for themselves by capturing Spanish ships. An especially famous Cornishman from this period is Richard Carew of Antony, author of the *Survey of Cornwall*, first published in 1602.

'TREVANION IS UP, AND GODOLPHIN IS NIGH,
AND HARRIS OF HAYNE'S O'ER THE RIVER:
FROM LUNDY TO LOOE, "ONE AND ALL" IS THE CRY,
AND THE KING AND SIR BEVILLE FOR EVER!'

Royal Institution of Cornwall

Later, in the Civil Wars in the mid seventeenth century, Cornish people were also fighting for their beliefs. Some were on the Roundhead or Parliamentarian side but many more supported the Royalist cause. Their leader in Cornwall was Sir Bevil Grenville, from Stowe in North Cornwall, who led the Cornish army to victory at Stamford Hill (near Bude) and at Lansdowne, near Bath in Somerset. Grenville was killed at the battle of Lansdowne but, despite this loss, the Cornish went on to capture Bristol. Grenville's right hand man at both Stamford Hill and Lansdowne was Anthony Payne, 'the Cornish Giant' as he was known. It is said that he later became a great favourite of King Charles II, and today a fine portrait of him by the artist Kneller (painted in 1680) hangs in the Royal Cornwall Museum in Truro.

Anthony Payne, 'the Cornish Giant'.

Bishop Jonathan Trelawny, celebrated in the famous Cornish song, is another significant Cornish figure from the seventeenth century. In 1688 he was imprisoned for refusing to obey James II's religious policies. Although the song tells us that the Cornish marched across the Tamar to secure his release, Trelawny was in fact acquitted by a jury that had tried him and was set free. There were great celebrations in Pelynt, Trelawny's native parish, and at neighbouring Looe.

In the early eighteenth century, Sidney Godolphin (from Godolphin, near Helston) was Lord High Treasurer under Queen Anne, a powerful position in the government which enabled him to play an important part in planning the Act of Union between England and Scotland as well as paying for Britain's wars against France. This was a time when Britain was emerging as a major commercial and naval power, and the Cornish played a significant role in this development. Naval commanders such as William Bligh (from St Tudy), Charles Vinnicombe Penrose (from Penryn), and Edward Boscawen (born at Tregothnan) saw service as explorers or in the pursuit of British maritime and Imperial interests. James Silk Buckingham, born at Flushing in 1786, became a journalist in India and later a Member of Parliament. He pressed for better ship designs and for higher standards of safety at sea, earning the nickname 'the Sailor's Friend'.

Sidney Godolphin, a shrewd and clever politician with great diplomatic skills. He was – according to Charles II – 'never in the way and never out of the way'.

Captain William Bligh

visited Tahiti in 1788 and again in 1791 to collect specimens of the breadfruit tree to take to the West Indies. During his first visit the crew of his ship **HMS Bounty** mutineed soon after the departure from Tahiti. Bligh and a few loyal sailors were cast off in an open boat but, in a superb feat of navigation and seamanship, they managed to reach Timor in the Dutch East Indies.

Science Photo Library

Born in a thatched cottage near South Crofty mine in the parish of Illogan, Richard Trevithick was famous as an inventor and engineer. In 1816 he visited Peru to supervise the operation of mining machinery he had designed and built for the Cerro de Pasco silver mines. He had many adventures in Latin America, on one occasion narrowly surviving an alligator attack. His invention of the self-propelled steam locomotive, trialled in Camborne on Christmas Eve 1801, is recalled in the song still sung at Cornish Rugby matches today:

The late eighteenth and nineteenth centuries were a time of industrial expansion, in Britain as a whole but particularly in Cornwall. A whole generation of Cornish inventors, scientists and engineers emerged to place Cornwall in the forefront of technological development. Richard Trevithick, born in Illogan in 1771, known everywhere as 'Cap'n Dick' or (like Anthony Payne before him) 'the Cornish Giant', developed the high-pressure boiler for beam engines used on Cornish mines and invented the steam locomotive.

TREVITHICKS,
PORTABLE STEAM ENGINE.

Catch me who can.

'GOIN' UP CAMBORNE 'ILL, COMIN' DOWN,
GOIN' UP CAMBORNE 'ILL, COMIN' DOWN,
THE 'OSSES STOOD STILL, THE WHEELS TURNED AROUN',
GOIN' UP CAMBORNE 'ILL, COMIN' DOWN,

WHITE STOCKINS, WHITE STOCKINS SHE WORE,
WHITE STOCKINS, WHITE STOCKINS SHE WORE,
WHITE STOCKINS SHE WORE, THE SAME AS BEFORE,
GOIN' UP CAMBORNE 'ILL, COMIN' DOWN.'

Mechanical Power Subduing
Animal Speed.

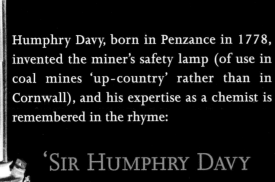

Penlee House Gallery and Museum, Penzance

Humphry Davy, born in Penzance in 1778, invented the miner's safety lamp (of use in coal mines 'up-country' rather than in Cornwall), and his expertise as a chemist is remembered in the rhyme:

'SIR HUMPHRY DAVY
ABOMINATED GRAVY
HE LIVED IN THE ODIUM
HAVING DISCOVERED SODIUM'

Amongst **Humphry Davy's** many achievements was his help in establishing the Zoological Society in 1825, the forerunner of today's London Zoo in Regents Park. He was also a Fellow and later President of the Royal Society, an association of distinguished scientists.

Another important Cornish scientist was John Couch Adams, born in Laneast in 1819, who discovered the planet Neptune and later became Professor of Astronomy at Cambridge. In those days, women were not encouraged to take an interest in scientific subjects but one who did was Caroline Fox, a member of the famous Fox family of Falmouth which included several inventors and important businessmen. Caroline Fox was born in 1819, and from 1835 kept a diary in which she recorded her meetings with scientists and famous thinkers such as John Stuart Mill.

Born in the remote moorland parish of Laneast, **John Couch Adams** rose to become President of the Royal Astronomical Society and Director of the University Observatory at Cambridge. However, he declined a knighthood and the prestigious post of Astronomer Royal

1851

Picking potatoes in Cornwall in the nineteenth century.
In those days many people viewed the Cornish with a prejudice that today we might label 'racist'.
In 1898, for example, Herbert S. Vaughan argued in his book *The British Road Book* that the Cornish were like the Irish, known for their 'dirt' and 'laziness'. This is what he wrote about Cornwall: *'There are thatched mud cabins here and there that might have been transplanted from Galway; hedges of stone, bogs and peat-stacks, pigs galore and a general aspect of dirt and happy laziness truly Irish. Also the people are very excitable and very kind-hearted, and in their dress often remind one of the Irish peasantry'.*

Mary Kelynack, born at Newlyn in 1777, is another well-known Cornishwoman from this period. But, unlike Caroline Fox, she did not come from an educated or wealthy background. Instead, she was a poor fisherman's wife. However, this did not prevent her from walking all the way, (or so it is said) to London and back in 1851 to see the Crystal Palace and satisfy her curiosity about the Great Exhibition of that year. More famous, perhaps, was Dame Fanny Moody Manners, the so-called 'Cornish Nightingale', born in Redruth in 1866, who became an opera star as well as a performer of popular songs such as 'Home, Sweet Home'. Her emotional rendering of 'Trelawny' at Johannesburg in South Africa in 1896 brought tears to the eyes of the many Cornish people who had gathered to hear her sing.

Despite the long list of the famous and the successful in nineteenth-century Cornwall, most ordinary people remained more or less invisible, living tough lives in the towns, on the land, amongst the mines, or in fishing and sea-faring communities. When we do have details of such ordinary folk, it is often because of some dreadful tragedy. Boys were often employed underground in the mines or at surface working the machinery. In 1850 James Clemo, aged 15, was killed deep in the West Caradon Mine, near St Cleer, when he fell 104 fathoms down a shaft. A few years before, in 1837, 12 year old George James was crushed to death by machinery at Wheal Vyvyan mine in Constantine. John Harris, the miner-poet born in 1820 at Bolenowe, near Camborne, caught the flavour of nineteenth-century Cornish mining in his often moving poetry:

Royal Institution of Cornwall, Truro

'Hast ever seen a mine? Hast ever been
Down it in its fabled grottoes, walled with gems,
And canopied with torrid mineral belts,
That blaze within the fiery orifice?
Hast ever, by the glimmer of the lamp,
Or the fast-waning taper, gone down, down,
Towards the Earth's dread centre, where wise men
Have told us that the earthquake is conceived,
And great Vesuvius hath his lava-house,
Which burns and burns forever, shooting forth
As from a fountain of eternal fire?
Hast ever heard, within this prison house,
The startling hoof of Fear? the eternal flow
Of some dread meaning whispering to thy soul?'

Women and girls were employed at surface at Cornish mines, sorting and grading the ore. These 'bal-maidens' acquired a reputation as being fiercely independent.

The independence and self-confidence of the **bal-maidens** sometimes annoyed their male critics. In the 1850s one such critic wrote that the hard toil on the mines was not proper work for women. Such work, he said, *'begets a want of modesty and delicacy [which] render them wholly unfit to perform and attend to those domestic duties which should constitute the comfort and charm of every home'*.

An example of the old **Cornish cottages** that in the nineteenth century reminded English visitors so much of Ireland or Brittany. Their inhabitants were regarded as a strange, remote people. In 1879 Robert Louis Stevenson wrote of the Cornish that *'Not even a Red Indian seems more foreign in my eyes'*. As late as 1952, in his book *Cornwall*, R. Thurston Hopkins could write about the Cornish in a way that today might be thought offensive: *'Yes, the Cornish are a strange and unquenchable race – today they are capable of loyal friendliness and often gracious actions, but we must not forget that we are meeting the descendants of folk who still have a leaven of paganism in their blood'*.

Billy Bray, the famous Cornish preacher.

This independence and individualism could also be seen in the activities of Cornwall's many Methodist local preachers, their reputations sometimes spreading far beyond the Tamar. Samuel Drew, born near St Austell in 1765, was a shoemaker who became an important Methodist preacher and thinker, writing books and essays on religion, politics and philosophy. Billy Bray, born at Twelveheads in 1794, was a much-loved eccentric whose preaching earned him an affectionate and enduring place in the history of Cornish Methodism. He died in 1868 and was buried in Baldhu.

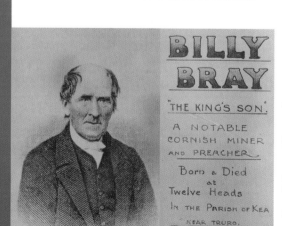

BILLY BRAY

'THE KING'S SON'.

A NOTABLE CORNISH MINER AND PREACHER.

Born & Died at Twelve Heads In the Parish of Kea near Truro.

Aged 73 Years

In the twentieth century, many Cornish men and women played major roles in the two World Wars. The Duke of Cornwall's Light Infantry was prominent in both and so too were Cornwall's part-time Territorial units, such as the Cornwall Fortress Royal Engineers which saw service in the First World War in great battles such as the Somme and Amiens. Others joined the Royal Air Force, and in the Second World War Cornishwomen served in the Women's Land Army as well as other units. Cornwall had always been an important source of personnel for the Royal Navy, and in the Second World War Lieutenant Commander Robert Hichens (from Flushing) was known as the 'Nelson of the Navy's little ships' for his daring exploits around the coasts of Britain in command of Motor Gun Boats. He won numerous medals for his bravery but was killed in a duel with an enemy gunboat off Felixstowe on 13 April 1943.

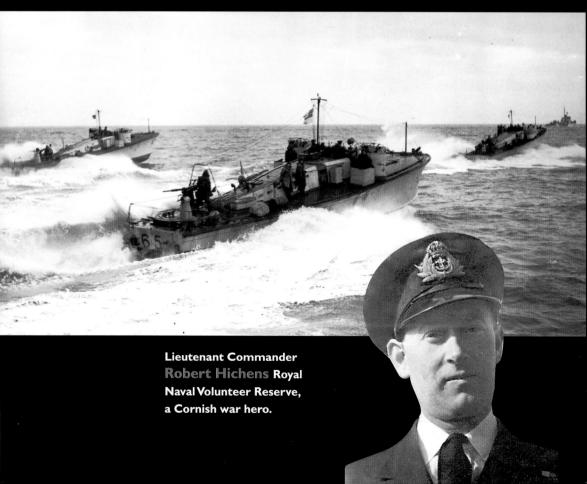

Lieutenant Commander Robert Hichens Royal Naval Volunteer Reserve, a Cornish war hero.

Raised originally in 1702 as a regiment of marines, the 'County Regiment' participated in the capture of Gibraltar in 1704 and in numerous other actions, notably the Defence of Lucknow in 1857 during the so-called Indian Mutiny. Later, in the Great War of 1914-1918, the Duke of Cornwall's Light Infantry raised fourteen battalions. No fewer than 4,282 of the regiment were killed and countless thousands were wounded. In the Second World War of 1939-1945, the DCLI, as it is often known, served in Europe and Africa as well as raising fourteen battalions of Home Guard to protect Cornwall.

The Keep and DCLI War Memorial

at Bodmin, home today of the Duke of Cornwall's Light Infantry Museum.

The Capture of Gibraltar in 1704.

The Defence of Lucknow in 1857.

The twentieth century also drew many people to Cornwall from outside. Writers and artists were attracted by Cornwall's sense of 'difference', and since 1945 they have been joined by many other people moving here in search of a different life style. Cornish people of note have thus included not only those born here of long-established Cornish families, such as the late David Penhaligon MP, but also newcomers and the children of newcomers – such as Dean Shipton, captain of Cornwall's victorious rugby football team at Twickenham in 1999, a true hero of modern Cornwall.

Dean Shipton, who led the Cornish rugby team to its victory over Gloucestershire (the 'Old Enemy') at Twickenham in 1999.

www.photo-point.co.uk

religion

'All these
Cornish
shores
are holy,
Here the Saints in prayer did dwell,
Raising font and altar lowly
Preaching far with staff and bell –
Piran,
Petroc,
Paul Aurelian,
Euny,
Samson,
Winwaloe.'

REV CANON MILES BROWN
HYMN TO THE CORNISH SAINTS

Cornwall is the 'Land of Saints'. Its placenames and church dedications echo the often half-remembered identities of Irish, Welsh, Breton and even indigenous Cornish holy men and women who are said to have established the 'Celtic church' here in the sixth century or thereabouts, and whose influence moulded Cornish Christianity as it developed in the Middle Ages (the period from about 1000 to 1500).

Holy wells, such as those at Sancreed and Madron, St Cleer and Dupath, and ancient chapels – like St Clether's on the River Inny or St Michael's on Rame Head – are reminders of those long departed days. So too are Cornwall's many Celtic crosses, such as St Piran's Cross in the dunes near Perranporth, dated to before 960AD. Fifteenth-century church towers give unity to an otherwise varied Cornish landscape – Morwenstow and Maker, Linkinhorne and Lanlivery, Constantine and Camborne – enduring markers of the Church in Cornwall.

Celtic crosses
in the Cornish landscape,
enduring memorials to
Christianity in Cornwall
and to Cornwall's place in
the Celtic world.

Cornubia: the painting by John Miller which vividly depicts Cornwall as
'The Land of Saints'. The original can be seen in Truro Cathedral.

Illustration by Joel Stewart, BA (Hons) Illustration course, Falmouth College of Arts

And yet, before the Age of Saints there was an older religion in Cornwall, a pagan belief which saw the handiwork of God or Gods everywhere in Nature. The wind in the trees, the power of the ocean, thunder in the skies; all these elements demanded worship in the Celtic pre-Christian religion of Cornwall. Stone circles and standing stones, inherited from even earlier pre-Celtic times, perhaps also played a role in this pagan religion. Some of these stones, inscribed later with the sign of the Cross, may have been co-opted by the first Christian missionaries. Many holy wells were no doubt once also pagan sites, their life-giving waters worshipped long before the coming of Christianity.

The arrival of Christianity in Cornwall is now thought to have occurred in the sixth century, the result of settlement here by Irish immigrants from the kingdom of Demetia in what is today southwest Wales. These settlers brought their Christian religion with them. Its spread can be detected in the Christian inscribed stones that can still be found across Cornwall, such as those at Lewannick which are inscribed in Latin and also in Ogham – the curious Irish stroke alphabet.

Trelew Menhir,
on the Penwith peninsula. Some ten feet high, this impressive standing stone was found to have calcined bones, charred wood, and baked clay at its foot when it was excavated in 1863.

Early Religious belief
saw the handiwork of God or Gods everywhere in Nature.

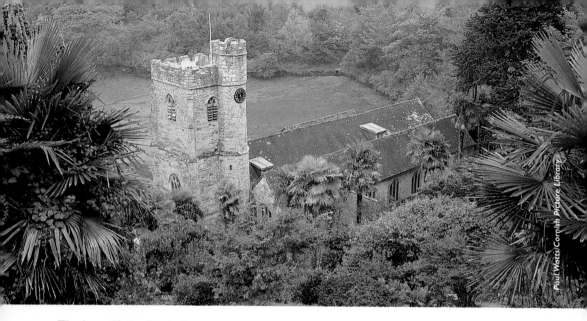

The beautifully situated church of St Just-in-Roseland, **said in legend to have been visited by Jesus and Joseph of Arimethea, and today a place of pilgrimage for Cornish and tourists alike.**

St Piran's Cross, **near Perranporth, dates from the 10th century.**

Alongside this archaeological evidence is a mass of legend, folklore and story-telling. One tale insists that, almost two thousand years ago, the boy Jesus came to Cornwall with his uncle – Joseph of Arimathea – to buy tin ingots. This little boy grew up to be a carpenter, a rebel, a teacher known as Jesus Christ who claimed to be the Son of God and whose death on the Cross is remembered in every Christian place of worship on Good Friday. Of course, we have no proof that Jesus came to Cornwall. But in the story of Joseph of Arimathea we see perhaps a dim folk memory of tin trading with the Mediterranean in ancient times and a remembrance that Christianity was brought to Cornwall from across the seas. Other tales are equally expressive, such as that which tells us that St Piran was cast into the sea, tied to a millstone, by the violent King Aengus of Munster in Ireland. But the millstone floated, and St Piran sailed across to Cornwall, landing on the beach at Perranporth. There he established his oratory or chapel, and he became the Patron Saint of Cornish Tinners and thus a Patron of Cornwall. His flag, a white cross on a black background, became the Cornish banner. In those days white upon black was thought to signify the triumph of Good over Evil; it also represented molten tin flowing from the black ore.

St Piran

Illustration by Roisin Mathews, BA (Hons) Illustration course, Falmouth College of Arts

St Michael's Mount

Bob Berry

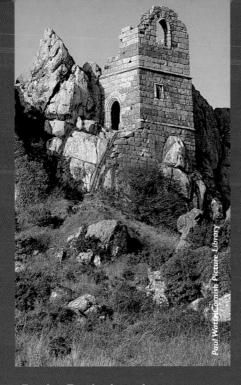

Paul Watts/Cornish Picture Library

Roche Rock chapel, near St Austell, is dedicated to St Michael.

Illustration by Louise Daykin, BA (Hons) Illustration course, Falmouth College of Arts

St Petroc is said to have helped an unhappy dragon who had a splinter in his eye.

St Petroc is another of Cornwall's Patrons, associated especially with North Cornwall – particularly Padstow and Bodmin. St Michael, the third of Cornwall's Patrons, is commemorated in high and holy places, such as St Michael's Mount and Roche Rock. In the Hal-an-tow ceremony early on the morning of Furry Day (May 8th) at Helston, the slaying of the dragon by St Michael is acted out each year, another depiction of the victory of Good over Evil.

Hal-an-tow is acted out each year at Helston's Flora or 'Furry' day.

The substantial masonry
of Glasney College.
Today it is difficult to
imagine this once
impressive institution
that stood at Penryn,
or to imagine the
scholarship that
existed within its walls.

By the Middle Ages the Church in Cornwall had come under the full authority of Rome. But Cornish ways still survived. Miracle plays, written in the Cornish language, were performed all across Cornwall, usually in an open-air 'plen-an-gwarry' or playing place. An early example is the *Ordinalia*, composed towards the end of the fourteenth century, probably at Glasney College at Penryn. The play charts the experience of Adam, from his 'fall' in the Garden of Eden to his eventual restoration to Heaven:

arluth ker bynyges os
a syv ioy gynef gothfos
an denses the thos th'en nef
as tas dev dre'n spyrys sans
th'n beys danvonas sylwyans
a huhon map dev a seyf

Or, in English:

Dear lord, ever blessed be
joy it brings to us to see
man brought to heaven again
The Father and Holy Ghost
redeemed a world that was lost
On high the Son will remain.

An artist's impression of
the *Ordinalia* being
performed at Piran Round.

Illustration by Norman Lister

National Portrait Gallery

In the reign of Henry VIII, however, the Church of England broke away from Rome, bringing the new religious ideas of Protestantism to Cornwall. Henry VIII died in 1547 but his work was continued by a government of Protestant councillors which guided the boy-king Edward VI. In Cornwall, there was much hostility to the new ways, especially to the use of English (instead of Latin) in church services. In a petition to the king, the Cornish declared that the new service was:

The boy-king Edward VI whose 'advisors' provoked the rebellion of Cornwall in 1549.

'LIKE A CHRISTMAS GAME . . . WE WILL HAVE OUR OLD SERVICE OF MATTINS, MASS, EVENSONG AND PROCESSION IN LATIN AS IT WAS BEFORE. AND SO WE THE CORNISH MEN (WHEREOF CERTAIN OF US UNDERSTAND NO ENGLISH) UTTERLY REFUSE THIS NEW ENGLISH'.

In 1549 the Cornish rose in rebellion against the Protestant religion and the English language. But they were defeated in a string of bloody battles in Devon. Suggestions that the new Prayer Book and Bible might be translated into the Cornish language were ignored and Glasney College, where the miracle plays had been written, was closed as part of the Protestant plan to dissolve the monasteries. As a result, the Cornish language began to decline.

1549

1595

Early in the morning of 23rd July 1595, four Spanish galleys landed a raiding party of two hundred men at Mousehole. They set fire to the village and to Paul church, as well as killing four locals who tried to stop them. Close to Mousehole is Merlin's Rock and so, it was said, was fulfilled the ancient Cornish prophecy:

After 1549 many Cornish people turned to the new Protestant religion, especially when the navy of Catholic Spain raided Mousehole and burned Penzance, but few adopted the more extreme form of Protestantism known as Puritanism. Some remained Roman Catholics, and were persecuted for their beliefs. In the Civil Wars in the mid-seventeenth century, most of the Cornish sided with the Royalists (the supporters of Charles I) against the Puritan Parliamentarians or 'Roundheads' as they were known.

EWRA TEYRE A WAR MEARNE MERLYN
ARA LESKY PAWLE, PENSANZ HA NEWLYN

THEY SHALL LAND ON THE ROCK OF MERLIN,
WHO SHALL BURN PAUL, PENZANCE AND NEWLYN

Later, in 1688, many Cornish supported Bishop Jonathan Trelawny when he was imprisoned in the Tower of London by James II, a Roman Catholic:

And shall Trelawny live?
Or shall Trelawny die?
Here's twenty thousand Cornish bold,
Will know the reason why!

1688

The Quaker Meeting House, at Come-to-Good near Feock, was built in 1710.

Some Cornish became members of the Society of Friends, or 'Quakers' as they were known, and still others became Baptists. But by the middle of the eighteenth century a new force was making itself felt in Cornwall, the Wesleyans or Methodists. In the 1740s John Wesley and his brother Charles had tackled what they saw as the shortcomings of the Church of England. They visited Cornwall no fewer than forty times, and although they were welcomed warmly by many ordinary Cornish folk – the miners, fishermen and farmers – they also encountered some opposition. Children used to shout:

'Mr Wesley's come to town...

John Wesley made frequent visits to Cornwall, and in 1781, at the age of 78 years, could still attract a congregation of 20,000 souls when he preached at Gwennap Pit.

In fact, John Wesley's followers – the Wesleyans and other Methodist sects such as the Bible Christians, Primitive Methodists and the New Methodist Connexion – built hundreds of chapels across Cornwall in the late eighteenth and nineteenth centuries. By the 1850s, Methodism had become the unofficial religion of Cornwall. It influenced every aspect of Cornish life, including the formation of male voice choirs and brass and silver bands, together with the composition of Cornish Carols by musicians such as Thomas Merritt. Women had an important part to play in the Methodist chapels, especially in the Bible Christians where many were preachers.

National Portrait Gallery

Gwennap Pit, at Gwennap, near Redruth, still exists today and remains the open-air 'Cathedral of Cornish Methodism'. In its hey-day, shown above, it could attract many thousands of worshippers, especially to the famous Whit-Monday services.

... To try to pull our churches down!'

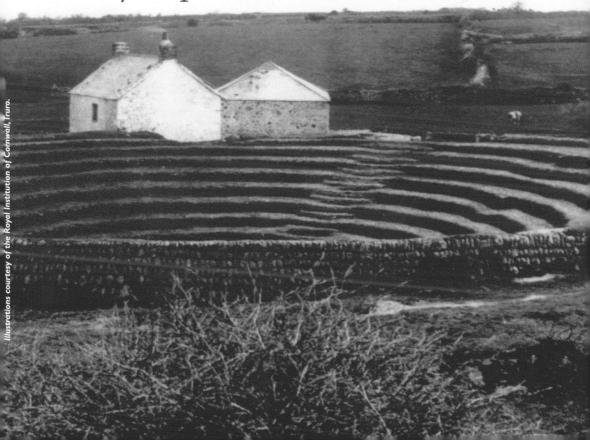

Late medieval stained-glass window panels from the church at St Neot.

However, despite the triumph of Methodism, there were those who considered that the Church of England in Cornwall should try to become more 'Cornish'. These people included the so-called Anglo-Catholic and Celtic Revivalists, who thought that the Church should look back to the Roman Catholic and Cornish traditions of the Middle Ages. They encouraged the remembrance of Celtic saints such as Piran and Petroc, and it was one early Revivalist – the famous Rev Robert Stephen Hawker of Morwenstow – who first made popular the now internationally celebrated Harvest Festival.

Others felt that Cornwall should have its own Cathedral, and in the 1870s the Cornish people raised a sum of money large enough for such a Cathedral to be built in Truro. Edward White Benson was appointed the first Bishop of Truro; he created the service of *Nine Lessons and Carols* which is now used in churches of the Anglican Communion at Christmas the world over.

The Royal Institution of Cornwall, Truro.

Edward White Benson, the first Bishop of Truro. This bust is now at the Royal Cornwall Museum in Truro.

Illustration courtesy of Truro Cathedral.

Some of the workmen engaged on the building of Truro Cathedral, around 1883.

In the twentieth century church attendance has declined. However, Christianity in Cornwall remains a vibrant force. The Methodists are strong when compared with other parts of Britain, and so too is the Anglo-Catholic strand of the Church of England, while some people have been attracted to the Orthodox Church. But there is also a determination that Christian churches should work 'together in Cornwall', putting aside their differences in belief and worship to confront Cornish problems and also to help resolve global issues such as the eradication of Third World debt.

At the same time, Cornwall has also become part of the new multicultural Britain. Judaism has long had a place in Cornish religion, and Islam, Hinduism and other beliefs have also found a home here. So too have the 'New Age' pagans, many of them attracted to Cornwall by its 'Celtic mysticism', with its holy wells, standing stones and other sacred spots. Like people of all religions and none, they find in Cornwall a timeless spirituality which is deeply healing.

The holy well at Madron is a sacred site visited by both Christians and 'New Age' pagans.

Brother Sun,
a contemporary
painting by artist
John Miller.

politics and power

Cornwall, as an entire state, hath at divers time enjoyed sundry... ...titles, of a kingdom, principality, duchy, and earldom.

RICHARD CAREW OF ANTONY
SURVEY OF CORNWALL
1602

**The Councils
of Cornwall
in the year 2000.**

North Cornwall

CORNWALL

Caradon

Restormel

Carrick

Penwith

Kerrier

At first glance, Cornwall might seem just like any county in England and Wales. We have our own County Council, with County Hall in Truro, and six District Councils: Penwith, Kerrier, Carrick, Restormel, North Cornwall and Caradon.

But scratch the surface, and things begin to look a little different. To begin with, there is the High Sheriff of Cornwall. In any other county the High Sheriff, the chief administrative officer whose duties are mainly ceremonial, is appointed by the Crown. In Cornwall, however, he or she is given the job by the Duke of Cornwall, who is also the Prince of Wales and the Heir to the Throne. This is a clue to Cornwall's distinctive political history, a story that can be traced back to the tenth century when in 936AD King Athelstan established the River Tamar as the border between Cornwall and his powerful Anglo-Saxon kingdom of Wessex.

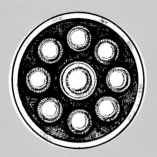

The **fifteen bezants** that appear today on the coats of arms of both the County and Duchy of Cornwall are said to derive from the ancient coins of Byzantium depicted on the shields of Richard, Earl of Cornwall (who died in 1272). In early examples the number of bezants is not fixed, and some examples show as many as twenty-two.

Early shield illustration courtesy of D. Endean Ivall.

Effigy of the Black Prince on his tomb in Canterbury Cathedral. He was the first Duke of Cornwall and victor over the French at the battles of Crécy and Poitiers.

Courtesy of Dean and Chapter of Canterbury Cathedral

Athelstan worked to unite the Anglo-Saxon kingdoms of England but he also sought to impose his authority on the neighbouring 'Britons' who lived in the Celtic lands of Cornwall and Wales. However, Cornwall, like Wales, continued to be treated as a place apart (in 944AD Athelstan's successor, Edmund, was known in Cornwall as 'King of the English and ruler of this province of the Britons'), and in the medieval period this gave rise to two important Cornish institutions – the Duchy of Cornwall and the Stannaries.

The Duchy of Cornwall grew out of an earlier Earldom, set up by the Normans, and was established in 1337 by Edward III who proclaimed his young son and heir (also called Edward) to be 'Duke of Cornwall'. Today, it is possible to point to the quite different activities of the Duchy of Cornwall (which owns more land outside Cornwall than within, and comprises the Prince of Wales' business interests) and Cornwall County Council, which is the local government authority. In medieval times, however, there was no such distinction, the Duchy providing such government as there was in Cornwall.

The Black Prince's doublet, helmet, shield, gauntlets and scabbard, preserved and on display in Canterbury Cathedral.

1337

Courtesy of Dean and Chapter of Canterbury Cathedral

The charter for the borough of **Launceston** granted by the Black Prince.

Much later, in 1855-57, the Duchy of Cornwall decided to write its own early history. Looking back to 1337, it found that 'the three Duchy Charters are sufficient in themselves to vest in the Dukes of Cornwall, not only the government of Cornwall, but the entire territorial dominion in and over the county'.

The original Charter of 1337 acknowledged that Cornwall was one of 'the remarkable places in our kingdoms', a remote land apart that might at any time rebel against London rule and which was also vulnerable to invasion from abroad. The newly-created Duchy recognised and gave expression to Cornwall's 'difference' but also provided a strong link with the government. Duchy castles at Launceston and at Tremation (near Saltash) guarded the border. Significantly, Tintagel Castle was built on the site of an earlier seat of Cornish royal power, dating back to the days when Cornwall was a separate kingdom. Restormel, the fourth Duchy castle, was constructed in the heart of the land actually owned by the Duchy of Cornwall, just a couple of miles up the River Fowey from the Duchy capital of Lostwithiel.

Replicas of the original clothing and armour of the **Black Prince** displayed at **Canterbury Cathedral.**

An engraving of **Launceston Castle,** near Saltash.

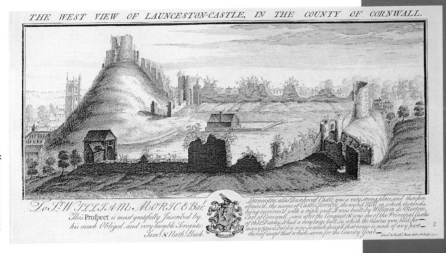

THE WEST VIEW OF LAUNCESTON-CASTLE, IN THE COUNTY OF CORNWALL.

At its foundation in 1337, the Duchy of Cornwall had also taken control of the Stannaries, an even older organisation which too had given Cornwall a degree of political independence. A Charter of 1201 had established four mining districts – or Stannaries – in which a separate system of Stannary Law was allowed to operate. These Stannaries were Foweymore (modern Bodmin Moor), Blackmore (the Hensbarrow Downs above St Austell), Tywarnhaile (the area around St Agnes and Truro), and Penwith-with-Kerrier in the far west. Added to this was the Stannary or Tinners' Parliament, whose wideranging powers included the right to overturn laws made by the London government in Westminster.

Illustration by Mark Short, BA (Hons) Illustration course, Falmouth College of Arts

In 1496 there was an argument between the Cornish Tinners and the Duke of Cornwall, a disagreement which led to the temporary suspension of the Stannaries. The Cornish were furious about this outside interference, and they were even more enraged in the following year, 1497, when taxes were levied by the government to pay for a war against Scotland. Under the leadership of Michael Joseph 'An Gof' ('the Smith') of St Keverne and Thomas Flamank of Bodmin, a Cornish army marched to London where it was defeated by the King's forces at the Battle of Blackheath. The Cornish promptly launched a second rebellion but got no further than Taunton before giving up.

The Battle of Blackheath.

1497

Paul Yockney

KESKERDH
KERNOW
500
1497-1997
CORNWALL
MARCHES ON!

In 1997, the 500th anniversary of the Cornish
Rebellion of 1497, thousands of Cornish
people participated in commemorative
events and celebrations. A great many joined
in the re-enacting march from St Keverne to
Blackheath (London), some even walking all
the way!

1997

Henry VII (or Henry Tudor, as he was known) imposed heavy fines on Cornwall, and the Cornish remained extremely angry. In the Cornish-language miracle play, *Beunans Meriasek* (the Life of St Meriasek), written at about this time, there is a struggle between Good and Evil in which the former eventually wins. Evil is represented in the play by the bad King Teudar, whose name is remarkably similar to that of Henry Tudor, and it may be that the Cornish were using *Beunans Meriasek* to criticise Henry VII. By 1508 Henry VII had decided that he needed to win back the loyalty of the Cornish, and he tried to do this in his so-called Charter of Pardon of that year. This Charter restored the Stannaries and gave back to the Cornish their degree of independence.

© National Portrait Gallery

The Cornish rebellions of 1497 were the greatest of the threats to Henry VII during his reign.

Only forty years later, however, the Cornish were again confronting the London government, this time over the Reformation in which new Protestant ways replaced the older Catholic traditions. The Cornish did not like the new ways and objected to the use of the English language in church services. Once again they rose in rebellion, in 1549 beseiging Exeter and fighting a series of bloody battles with the King's forces in Devon. The Cornish were driven back across the Tamar, and this time the government took harsh measures to teach Cornwall a lesson. Many rebels were hanged or otherwise slaughtered.

Memorial at St Ives to John Payne, mayor, who was executed for his part in the 1549 rebellion.

From original illustrations by Roger Penhallurick, The Royal Institution of Cornwall, Truro

These Cornish pennies from the early 1800s emphasise both the sense of independence felt by Cornwall and the power of its mining industry under the jurisdiction of the Stanneries.

Although some Cornish did cling to the Roman Catholic religion, after 1549 many people in Cornwall – especially the gentry – became enthusiastic supporters of Protestantism. Cornwall became the 'front line' in the wars with Catholic Spain, and the loyalty of Cornish gentlemen was rewarded by the government with the granting of numerous borough charters. Boroughs with charters were allowed their own Members of Parliament, and soon Cornwall had an astonishing forty-four MPs in the House of Commons at Westminster – only one fewer than the forty-five MPs given to Scotland at the Act of Union in 1707.

Charles I, from a portrait at Antony House, near Torpoint. The Royalist cause recognised its debt to Cornwall and the Cornish, the Royalist journal *Mercurius Aulicus* writing approvingly that:

'CORNWALL (WHICH IS LITTLE WALES BEYOND ENGLAND) PROVED THEMSELVES TRUE BRITTAINES, WHEN NO ENGLISH COUNTY STOOD INTIRELY FOR HIS MAJESTIE'

However, the Cornish resistance to interference from outside had hardly diminished. In the Civil Wars that raged throughout the British Isles in the mid-seventeenth century, Cornwall played a distinctive role. Although a few Cornish gentry supported the Parliamentarian or 'Roundhead' side in the Civil Wars, most Cornish people were 'Royalists' and supported the King (Charles I) in his struggle with Oliver Cromwell. Wales, Ireland, Scotland and the North of England were also Royalist areas, while southern England and the Midlands tended to be Parliamentarian. When Roundhead armies attempted to enter Cornwall in early 1643 they were soundly defeated by Cornish Royalist forces at Braddock Down, near Lostwithiel, and at Stamford Hill, Stratton near Bude.

1643

Today, the 'Sealed Knot' re-enacts the battle of Stamford Hill and other clashes between Royalists and Roundheads in Cornwall.

Eventually, the Parliamentarians won the Civil Wars. Charles I was executed and Oliver Cromwell was made Lord Protector, the new head of government in London. However, Cornwall was one of the last places to hold out for the Royalist cause. The Cornish rebelled against the new Parliamentarian government in 1648, and the Royalist garrison on the Isles of Scilly did not surrender until 1654. Cromwell abolished the Duchy of Cornwall and the Stannaries, as well as reducing the number of Cornish MPs to twelve, but when in 1660 (after Cromwell's death) Charles II was invited to take the Crown, all this was restored.

The Stannaries remained important for many years after. Although the Stannary Parliament last met in 1753, the system of Stannary Law was in active use until the late nineteenth century, a result of the great increase in copper and tin mining in that period. The Duchy of Cornwall also remained important, but less as an aspect of government and more as a source of income for the Prince of Wales. Many of the forty-four Cornish seats at Westminster survived until the Great Reform Act of 1832 when, as part of the attempt to establish fairer Parliamentary representation throughout Britain, the number was again reduced to twelve.

However, at the same time that these old symbols of Cornish politics and power were disappearing or changing, so new symbols were emerging. The most important of these was the relationship that grew up between Methodism and the Liberal Party in Cornwall during the nineteenth century. The Methodists, who had broken away from the Church of England, were religious 'Radicals' and they were attracted to the political 'Radicals' of the Liberal Party. They supported reforms designed to improve the living conditions of ordinary people and to give more people the vote in Parliamentary elections.

© National Portrait Gallery

Oliver Cromwell's Roundhead troops took a dim view of the Cornish, Welsh and Irish, describing them all as 'pagans' and 'heathens'. One wrote of 'Hellish Cornwall' and another thought that *'the men of Cornwall are very heathens, a corner of ignorants, and atheists, drained from the mines'.*

The *West Briton* newspaper, founded in 1810, was set up as a voice for Radical opinion. In those days it covered the whole of Cornwall, and amongst its supporters were members of a benevolent squirarchy such as Sir Christopher Hawkins and the well-known Rashleigh, Trelawny and Molesworth families.

The links between the Cornish Methodists and the Liberals were so close that when, in the years after the First World War, support for the Liberal Party declined in much of Britain it remained strong in Cornwall. When, in the 1980s, the Liberals became the Liberal Democrats, they found that they still had extensive Cornish support.

The Conservative Party, meanwhile, discovered that it could best appeal to Cornish voters when concentrating on local issues. This was especially true in the years after the Second World War, when the most popular Conservative MPs were those with strong local connections. For much of the period after 1945, the Parliamentary representation of Cornwall was dominated by the Conservatives, although they did not win any Cornish seats in the General Election of 1997.

The Labour Party was slow to develop in Cornwall, partly because the Liberals had remained the main opponents of the Conservatives, and partly because the rapid decline of the Cornish mining industry at the end of the nineteenth century had robbed Cornwall of the conditions in which Labour might expect to thrive. However, the Labour Party was able to grow in areas where industrial activity had survived and, like the Conservatives, its most successful politicians were those with local roots or sympathies who were prepared to concentrate on local issues.

Harold Hayman,
the veteran Cornish-
born Labour MP who
held Falmouth and
Camborne from his
election in 1950 to his
death in 1966.

The very first front page
of the West Briton
newspaper, published on
July 20th 1810.

Courtesy of Cornwall and Devon Media Ltd.

The West Briton

AND CORNWALL ADVERTISER.

JULY 20, 1810.] Printed and Published by JOHN HEARD, No. 30, Boscawen-Street, TRURO. [No. 1.---Price 6½d.

[ON] THE LATE SESSION OF [P]ARLIAMENT.

[From] a London Paper.]

[...] the proceedings of last Session
[...]t be highly interesting, if not
[...]g to all those, who are luda-
[...]e character of the British Le-
[...]w that we have reached the
[...]ogation, in the language of
[...] the vantage ground," from
[...] surveyed in their fullest in-
[...]ter upon a review of the sena-
[...]ur Representatives, with all
[...]s due to their station, but, at
[...] that freedom of discussion,
[...]guishing characteristic of an
[...] Such tempered conduct we
[...] to the critical situation at
[...] arrived, or to which it has
[...]d, if a resolution must at last
[...]ne so likely to be supported
[...]at which has been adopted

[...] of as great * a Statesman as
[...]e present Cabinet, and who
[...]f England at a juncture ap-
[...]s, and certainly as glorious,
[...]our fate to live, that " Exe-
[...]e destroyed not by a Pan-
[...]sibility of our ruin, and by
[...]s then admitted by one per-
[...]judge; and the opinion, we
[...]ered, not in the warmth of
[...]pectation of paradox, but so-
[...]h apophthegm, which, from
[...]uth, was constantly in the
[...]ous character. Experience
[...]lation to support his theory.
[...]ceeding reign a Parliament
[...]h to confer the legislative
[...]ere Proclamations of the
[...]ed, as he was, with the de-
[...]ture, and its proneness to
[...]t conclude, although no
[...]e, as to the *possibility*, that
[...] Parliament might exist, of
[...]uld be the soul and animat-
[...] how destitute of talent or
[...]e; which would confound
[...]ll with attachment to the
[...]he basest sacrifice of duty
[...] with the imposing mask of
[...] regard public measures,
[...]e public, but the Minister,
[...]nm from the impulse of
[...] independent exercise of
[...]become the mere organ of
[...]werful than prerogative,
[...], every change in the at-
[...]—having been *forced* so
[...]
[...] *the People*, he could enter
[...] betraying their trust, and
[...]ight become of the forms
[...]e ruin of England must be
[...]ce. But quitting, for the
[...] of Lord Burleigh, which
[...] digression, let us resume
[...]ct, with which we have a
[...]tant connection.

[...], invidious at the present
[...] upon the manner in which
[...]lleagues came into office.
[...] always expressed great
[...] shyness at any allusion,
[...] their political life. The
[...] on that occasion, acted
[...]riotic principles of Blake,
[...]uty of a man to fight for
[...]er hands the government
[...] " It is not for us," said he,
[...] but to keep foreigners
[...]ordingly, the People of
[...]rror of a foreign force,
[...] with invasion, turned all
[...]wly-formed Cabinet, and
[...] scrupulously its claims
[...]ced great reliance on the
[...]vigour of an Administra-
[...]d in their declamation
[...]lindness, and debility of
[...]t the present Ministers
[...]rent manner from their
[...]il days; that they have
[...]s, been generously pro-
[...]f the public money, and
[...]prizes of great moment,
[...], is most certain; but if
[...]our foreign and domestic
[...] fairly doubted, whether,
[...]ects, the People of the
[...]on much higher ground
[...]e wise, provident, and
[...]rtook the management
[...]hat they have been uni-
[...]eir measures would be
[...]d be false; but the mis-
[...]r success has been most
[...] military actions during
[...]ninsula, is where they
[...]eared; whereas, failure
[...]s, where the Ministers
[...]y active. That this is
[...]mation, but downright
[...]y any one, who looks
[...]d examines his ideas of
[...] of the war. No man
[...]st degree, the honour
[...]alavera to the Premier;
[...] Walcheren Expedition
[...]oncentrated splendours
[...]e Minister. To Lord
[...]n reference to that me-
[...] *ex ida laude centurio,*
[...]*, nihil turma decerpit.—*
[...]*m humanarum Domine*
[...]*rtatem gloriæ non effert*
[...]*, ac proprium fatetur.*
[...]*n sapientia commiserit,*
[...]*illitur.* With all due de-
[...]t that this language is
[...] the Noble Lord as to
[...]*almost literal* version of
[...]

the passage will prove. " No, no, my Lord, you can throw no share of the blame upon the General or the Admiral, the Colonel or the Captain, the Army or the Fleet. Nay, Fortune herself, who hath such broad shoulders, and who is so ready to lend them for the support of blunders, that the vanity of mankind is unwilling to take upon itself, will not serve your turn upon this occasion. Like your late Constituents, she has left your Lordship in the lurch. She gives you full credit and complete allowance for this far-famed and much-laughed-at expedition. Nor will all your circumlocution and " distinctness of statement" prevail with the People of the United Empire to confound, out of compliment to you, rashness with wisdom, or chance with design."

The mind of the public was astounded by a series of disasters, the cause of which was easily to be traced to the Ministers themselves; but yet, in that temper, which has always distinguished the inhabitants of the British Islands, they looked to the meeting of Parliament for information and redress. The words of Lord Porchester were strictly descriptive of the feelings of the people: " the expectation of the country," said his Lordship, " is directed towards us;" at which expression, a sardonic laugh was heard from the Treasury Bench, as if in derision of the confidence of the country, and in anticipation of its disappointment. We will venture to say that, if such was the meaning of their irony, their foresight has been justified in the event. On the 23d of January, Parliament was opened, or, to adopt the military language of Lord Viscount Castlereagh upon a former occasion, " the Parliamentary Campaign began." It is our purpose, in pursuance of the soldier-like metaphor, to give a detailed account of the events which have occurred during this Campaign, in which, without any figure or hyperbole, we may safely assert, that the British Constitution has suffered more severe and dangerous wounds, than ever have been inflicted upon her since the period of the Revolution.

The Speech from the Throne, on the meeting of Parliament, avowedly the composition of Ministers, contained a brief recapitulation of the political events that had occurred during the period of the recess,—the fatal termination of the Campaign on the Danube,—the scandalous failure of the expedition to Walcheren,—the purchase of a peace by Sweden, without consulting England as to the terms of the bargain,—the glorious, but ineffectual victory of Talavera,—the dubious state of the two nations upon the Peninsula,—and the late, tardy, and unwilling adoption of that, which ought to have been the very first measure, after a strictly popular insurrection, the assembly of the Cortez in Spain,—and the threatened rupture with the United States of America. Each of these topics had undergone ample discussion among the people, and [upon] most of them the public mind was made up.

(*To be continued.*)

ELEGANT PIANO-FORTES TO LEND.

HANDSOME new PIANO-FORTES, with additional Keys, may be had at Tregoning's Repository, Truro, at 10s. 6d. per month.

SHARES in MINES.

TO be SOLD, One Sixty-fourth SHARE in CARN HOT MINE. Apply to the Printer of this Paper.
Dated July 14, 1810.

SHARES in MINES.

TO be SOLD, SHARES in WHEAL LIBERTY MINE. Terms known on application to Mr. Jas. Stephens's, St. Agnes; or to Mrs. Simmons, Redruth.
Dated July 13, 1810.

SHARES in MINES.

FOR SALE by PRIVATE CONTRACT, COST-ALL-LOST TIN-MINE, in the parish of Roach, from One to Thirteen 128th SHARES. Nearly £1300 has been received for Tin sold from this Mine, between the 12th of April and the 20th of June last, and there is at present at surface a quantity valued at a much larger sum. This Mine is worked by two water-wheels, and the greatest depth of the levels is only twenty fathoms.

NORTH DOWN COPPER-MINE, One 28th SHARE.

WHEAL CHANCE, One 192d SHARE.

TRELUGA, One 64th SHARE.

These Mines are all very promising and well worthy the attention of those desirous to adventure.

Further particulars may be known, by application to the different Agents; or to Mr. Thomas Whitford, Truro, the proprietor.

Truro, 17th July, 1810.

CAUTION

Against unlawfully sending, carrying, and conveying Letters.

GENERAL POST-OFFICE.

By the Act of the 42d Geo. III. 81.

IT is Enacted, that no Person whatsoever shall send, or cause to be sent, or tender or deliver in order to be sent, otherwise than by the Post, or by the authority of the Postmaster-General or his Deputies, or to the nearest or most convenient Post-Town, to be from thence forwarded by the Post, any Letters, on pain of forfeiting for every offence 5l. to be recovered with Costs by any person who will inform and sue in any Court of Record at Westminster—one moiety to the King, and the other to the Informer.

Under this Law a person carrying a Letter may inform against a person sending one.

There is an exception in the Act as to Letters which concern Goods sent by Common Carriers, so as they are sent with and for the purpose of being delivered with the Goods without *hire, reward, or advantage* for receiving or delivering.

Carriers, Masters of Stage-Coaches, Coachmen, Owners, Masters or Commanders of Vessels, or Passengers, Watermen, and Bargemen, are liable to the penalty of 5l. besides Costs, for every Letter which they shall receive, carry or deliver, even without hire or reward.—And to a penalty of 100l. for every week that such practice shall be continued: and these penalties may be sued for *by any person who will inform.*

The Postmaster-General *hereby give Notice*, that all persons acting contrary to Law will be proceeded against with the utmost severity, and due encouragement will be afforded to persons who shall give information.

By command of his Majesty's Postmaster-General,

FRANCIS FREELING, Secretary.

WHEAT and HOPS.

NOW landing and on SALE, a small Cargo of French WHEAT, at 25s. per Bushel; also, a few Pockets of Prime HOPS; well worth the attention of Brewers and Dealers, as from the unfavourable appearance of the Hop Plantations a considerable advance is expected.

Apply at the Warehouse of Messrs. T. Tuck and Son, Truro, July 17, 1810.

To PARENTS and GUARDIANS.

WANTED, an APPRENTICE in the MERCERY TRADE, situated in one of the Western Towns of the county.—Terms known by application. Letters (post-paid) to the West Briton Office.

To PARENTS and GUARDIANS.

WANTED,

AN APPRENTICE to the PRINTING and STATIONARY Business. A Lad of respectable Connexions will be treated with on moderate Terms, on Application (Letters post-paid) to the Printer.

Truro, 18th July, 1810.

PICKED up at Sea, some time since, a Long SPAR.—Any person proving the property may have it, on paying the necessary expences, on application to Richard Brown, Truro.

Truro, July 18, 1810.

TO JOURNEYMEN CARPENTERS.

WANTED, THREE JOURNEYMEN CARPENTERS. Steady men will meet with constant employment and good wages on application to Mr. Wm. Downe, St. Clement-street, Truro.

Dated July 11, 1810.

TRURO HUMANE INSTITUTION.

THE first Half-yearly Meeting of THE HUMANE INSTITUTION, will be held at the Town-Hall, on Monday, the twenty-third day of this month, at eleven o'clock in the forenoon. The attendance of the Subscribers is particularly requested.

Truro, 18th July, 1810.

TRURO.

A HOUSE FOR SALE.

TO be SOLD by PRIVATE CONTRACT, for the residue of 99 years, determinable on the deaths of three healthy lives, all that neat and convenient newly-erected DWELLING-HOUSE, in King-street, Truro, now in the occupation of Mr. John Clemow, the proprietor, to whom application for particulars may be made; or to Mr. John Tyack, Charles-street, Truro.

N. B. The Premises are exceedingly eligible for a Shop of any kind.

Truro, 17th July, 1810.

Mr. BUDD's

COMMERCIAL and MATHEMATICAL SCHOOL,

Will re-commence on MONDAY the 23d of this month.

Mr. BUDD having engaged as an ADDITIONAL ASSISTANT, a person fully conversant with the business and management of a School, and being determined to make no engagement which shall prevent the continuance of those personal exertions which have hitherto secured the approbation of his friends, relies with confidence upon their kindness for a continuance of that support which he has hitherto so amply experienced.

Truro, July 18, 1810.

NOTICE to DEBTORS & CREDITORS.

ALL Persons who stand indebted to the Estate of the late Mr. JOHN DYMOND, Brewer, of Launceston, are desired to pay the same to Mr. Jas. Dymond, the Executor, or to Mr. John Roe, Chandler, Mr. Evry, Haberdasher, or Mr. W. Pearce, Woolstapler, the Trustees of the said John Dymond, on or before the 20th of October next: And all Persons having Demands on the aforesaid Estate, are desired to send in their Claims to the same, that they may be settled before the 20th of October next, as after that period no Demand can be adjusted or attended to.

Launceston, July 14, 1810.

CORNWALL.

CHURCH PREFERMENT.

TO be SOLD by PRIVATE CONTRACT, the Next PRESENTATION to the RECTORY of St. EWE, pleasantly situated near the South coast, of the computed annual value of five hundred pounds, exclusive of the Glebe Lands, which consist of about 76 acres, a commodious Dwelling-house, with Gardens, Orchards, &c.

The present Incumbent is about 35 years of age and his health precarious.

For further information, apply to Messrs. Rashleigh and Coode, St. Austell.

Dated 12th July, 1810.

BOROUGH OF PENRYN.

CAPITAL PREMISES FOR TRADE.

TO be LET by PRIVATE CONTRACT, for 7 or 14 years, with immediate possession, all that large and elegant SHOP, with a handsome HOUSE; consisting of two kitchens, sitting parlour, handsome dining-room, and six lodging-rooms; together with the Stable, Warehouses, Garden, &c. behind the same.

These Premises are situated opposite the Market-house, and are admirably calculated for a large wholesale or retail trade, and by letting genteel lodgings all the rent may be paid.

Further information may be had from Mr. Wm. Cock, Penryn, Builder; and by letters (post-paid) to Mr. Richards, the Proprietor, Architect, Truro.

ALSO,

To be SOLD by AUCTION, on Saturday, the 28th inst. by three o'clock in the afternoon, near the Cavalry Barracks, Truro, about 34 Tons of excellent Old HAY. (*one property.*)

Dated June 17th, 1810.

STATE LOTTERY.

NEW SCHEME.

Only 4000 Numbers—5 Prizes of £20,000—Tickets much cheaper than in the last Lottery, and not Three Blanks to a Prize.

THERE being 1000 Numbers *less*, and *one* Prize of Twenty Thousand Pounds *more*, than in the last Lottery, it must be clear that the chance of each Ticket or Share is increased *one-fifth*, and in addition to the superior advantages in the Scheme, the *prices* are considerably *lower* than in the last Lottery; though, from the circumstances of the Lottery, there can be little doubt of an advance of price before the Drawing, viz. 19th of October next,

SWIFT & Co.

Contractors with Government for the present Lottery, respectfully inform their friends and the public, that the Tickets and Shares are on sale, in great variety, at their Offices in London, viz.—

No. 12, CHARING-CROSS;
No. 11, POULTRY;
No. 31, ALDGATE HIGH-STREET;

Where, in the Last Lottery, No. 1,467,

A PRIZE OF £20,000,

Was sold in Sixteen Sixteenth Shares.

Also by their Agents,

Mr. TREGONING, Truro,
Mr. PEARCE, Penryn,

APPRENTICE WANTED.

MR. Joseph Philp, of Liskeard, SADLER, HARNESS-MAKER, &c. is in want of an APPRENTICE, who will be treated in every respect as one of the family. Letters must be post-paid, and a small premium will be expected.

Liskeard, 25th July, 1810.

MICHELL, STACEY, COCK & MICHELL,

BRANDY MERCHANTS,

REDRUTH,

Beg leave to offer the Public,

EXCELLENT OLD PORT WINES,

ON THE BEST TERMS.

☞ GENUINE SPIRITS, of all sorts.

Dated Redruth, July 16, 1810.

HEARD and PENALUNA,

PRINTERS AND BOOKBINDERS,

NEAR THE FISH-STRAND,

FALMOUTH,

Return their most grateful Acknowledgments to their Friends for the very liberal Support which they have received, and beg to inform them that they still continue the Business as above, and humbly solicit their future Patronage.

Falmouth, July 19, 1810.

TO BE SOLD,

A LEASEHOLD TENEMENT, in the parish of Kea, adjoining to Restronguet Water, and within three miles of the borough of Truro; consisting of two Cottages, a Barn, Stable, and convenient Sheds, with about 15 Acres of very improvable Land, divided into twelve Enclosures, exclusive of one Acre planted with thriving young Fruit Trees, of the best quality.

If not before privately disposed of, a SURVEY will be held for the same, on Saturday, the 29th September ensuing, at ten o'clock in the forenoon, upon the Premises, where further particulars may be known; or at the West Briton Office, Truro.

Dated July 17, 1810.

UNREDEEMED PLEDGES.

TO BE SOLD BY AUCTION,

ON Thursday, the 26th day of July, 1810, at the house of Mr. Wm. Geny, Pawnbroker, in Falmouth, a large quantity of UNREDEEMED PLEDGES; consisting of Plate, Watches, Wearing Apparel, &c. The following are the months when pledged, and numbers of each respective lot. 1808, *June*, Nos. 28, 45, 57, 60. *July*, Nos. 2, 18, 22, 23, 24, 27, 30. *Aug.* Nos. 13, 19, 30, 41, 45. *Sept.* Nos. 1, 33, 38, 47, 68. *Oct.* Nos. 49, 66. *Nov.* Nos. 16, 18, 22, 28, 55, 63, 64. *Dec.* Nos. 17, 70. 1809, *Feb.* Nos. 18, 24, 32, 47, 61. *March*, Nos. 11, 71. *April*, Nos. 12, 22, 27, 41, 52, 59, 70, 82. *May*, Nos. 2, 13, 41, 42, 74, 75, 78. *June*, Nos. 1, 4, 11, 16, 17, 21, 22, 23, 24, 27, 43, 59, 63. *July*, Nos. 1, 6, 11, 13, 14, 15, 19, 24, 27, 31, 34, 36, 38, 40, 43, 50, 53.

Falmouth July 12, 1810.

PLYMOUTH NEWSPAPER.

THE PLYMOUTH CHRONICLE Newspaper, published on Tuesdays at Plymouth, and which has now been established two years, contains a detail of all the interesting news of that important naval arsenal, together with the arrivals and sailings of the shipping, and the latest London intelligence to Sunday evening six o'clock. The PLYMOUTH CHRONICLE, to an extensive circulation, offers to advertisers the greatest advantages, a number being sent to all the seaport and large towns of England and Ireland, to the West-Indies, and our Colonies abroad, as well as dispersed through the Navy.

The PLYMOUTH CHRONICLE is printed and published by C. Redding, Barrack-street, Frankfort-Place, Plymouth, to whom and where all Orders and Advertisements are requested to be sent, when they will be punctually attended to.

Plymouth, July 17, 1810.

CORNWALL

AGRICULTURAL SOCIETY.

THE next EXHIBITION of CATTLE, &c. will be held at Helston, on Tuesday July 24, 1810, at Eleven o'Clock precisely, when the following Premiums will be given:—

	£.	s.	d.
For the best Bull	5	0	0
For the 2d best ditto	2	0	0
For the best Ram free for all England	5	0	0
For the best Ram yeaned in Cornwall	2	0	0
For the best Hog Ram yeaned in Cornwall	2	0	0
For the best Ram yeaned in Cornwall, the property of a Farmer of this County, getting his livelihood solely by farming, an Estate, in his own actual possession at Rack-Rent or otherwise, of not greater annual value than 200l.	5	0	0
For the 2d best ditto	1	0	0
For the best Boar	2	2	0
For the 2d best ditto	1	0	0

To be entered at the Angel Inn, Helston, or with the Secretary, at Bodmin, 14 days before the Exhibition.

Dinner at the Angel Inn, at 2 o'Clock, where the company of Gentlemen, Farmers, and others inclined to promote the object of this Society is desired.

By order of the Society,

JOHN WALLIS, Secretary.

London, June 26, 1810.

TO THE PUBLIC.

THE unexampled patronage which we experienced at this period of the last year, (when we had the honour of laying before the Public the Chancellor of the Exchequer's Plan for the prevention of insurance,) has induced us to contract for the present Lottery; and we confidently hope, that the Scheme now submitted for the public approbation, will entitle us to a continuation of the patronage and support we then received. We have the satisfaction to add, that having taken this Lottery at a cheaper rate than that at which the last Lottery was purchased, we are enabled to bring out the Tickets and Shares at much less Prices.

RICHARDSON, GOODLUCK & Co.
SWIFT & Co.

STATE LOTTERY,

To be Drawn the 19th of October, 1810.

NEW SCHEME.

5	of £20,000	are	£100,000
5	2,000		10,000
5	1,000		15,000
10	500		5,000
30	100		3,000
50	50		2,500
100	25		2,500
4,800	15		72,000
4,000 Numbers.			£220,000

FIVE TICKETS OF EACH NUMBER.

The Numbers of the Tickets in this Lottery are reduced to 4,000; and as the Scheme contains an additional Capital of £20,000, it must be obvious that the Chance of gaining a £20,000 Prize is increased One Fifth; and those who wish to adventure for larger sums have now an opportunity of gaining Forty, Sixty, Eighty, or even One Hundred Thousand Pounds! by purchasing two or more Tickets of one Number.

ABRAHAM's LITHONTRIPTIC.

AS a further proof of the efficacy of this Medicine, we have inserted the following:—

Sir,—I think it my duty to request you to make my case known for the benefit of those that may be afflicted with the like dreadful disease. I have been severely afflicted with the gravel upwards of five years, during which time I have not omitted taking such medicines recommended by several of the faculty, and had been advised to go to Bath, with all these I have complied, but without effect; fortunately having seen your valuable Lithontriptic advertised, of which I have taken six bottles, by which I have found a perfect cure. It is now upwards of two years since, and have had not the least symptoms of return.

I am, Sir, &c. C. F. Andrew.

Narrough, June 18, 1810.

This Medicine is sold wholesale at Messrs. Barclay and Son's, 95, Fleet-Market London; by the Proprietor at Breage, near Helston, who will give advice gratis; by Mrs. Thomas, Truro; and by [...] the venders of medicines in the kingdom.

HEALTH AND LONGEVITY.

Dr. James's Analeptic and Antibilious Pills

THE celebrity of the ANALEPTIC PILLS, as a general preservative of health, is become universal, from their efficacy in those complaints which continually disturb the human frame; such as colds, rheumatisms, head-achs, indigestions, and other diseases of the stomach and bowels, which arise from the vicissitudes of our climate, or from indulgence in the luxuries of life; and these salutary effects are produced by gently opening the pores by night, and the body by day, without requiring any particular regimen or confinement. But though the Analeptic Pills are also very serviceable in bilious and other deep-seated disorders, yet being designed as a mild purgative only, and therefore not always sufficiently active, the Antibilious Pills have been recommended in aid by an eminent Physician, in all complaints of the liver, as well as in other internal diseases.

Sold only by F. Newberry and Sons, No. 45, St. Paul's Church-yard, London; sold also by their appointment, by Cookworthy and Co., Haydon and Co., Jackson and Rees and Co., Plymouth; viz. the Analeptic Pills, price 4s. 6d. a Box, or six in one large Box for 1l. 4s.; and the Antibilious Pills, price 2s. 9d. a Box, duty included. —Observe that the words " F. Newberry, No. 45, St. Paul's," are engraved in the stamps.

For RHEUMATISMS, SPRAINS, CHILBLAINS, &c.

Dr. STEERS's OPODELDOC.

In the stamp round each bottle are engraved the words " F. Newberry, No. 45, St. Paul's," and those without this distinction are spurious.

THE success of this Medicine has given rise to a great number of counterfeits, as well as to a variety of Embrocations, Essences, Liniments, &c. some of which are so hot and strong, as often to excoriate, to cause blisters, or even to contract the sinews; and others are so weak as to be of no effect; but this Opodeldoc, by its happy combination, by the union of efficacy and safety, will ever maintain its wonted eminence and superiority. By its warm, penetrating, and attenuating qualities, it is a most excellent remedy for external rheumatisms; and by its strengthening powers, it speedily restores the parts which are injured by bruises and sprains; it is of great service in cramps, or numbness; in stiffness or weakness of the joints; and also in promoting circulation in the limbs when in a paralytic state; it is likewise particularly useful for chilblains, and if used in time, will prevent their breaking; but in this complaint a little of it should be dissolved in a spoon, and applied warm.

Sold only by F. Newberry, No. 45, St. Paul's, London, price 2s. 6d. each bottle, duty included; and, by their appointment, by Cookworthy, Fox and Co., Haydon and Co., Jackson, and Rees and Curtis, Plymouth.

Dr. TAYLOR's

ANTI-SPASMODIC PILLS.

A certain cure of the Epilepsy, or Falling Sickness, Convulsion Fits, Hysteric and Paralytic Affections, Cramp in the Stomach, &c. and an infallible antidote of that mortal malady the Apoplexy.

IT has been asserted from respectable authority, that a great majority of cases of epilepsy are incurable by any remedy that has yet been discovered. And indeed some of the medicines prescribed by the faculty for this dreadful complaint, are not only inefficacious, but often hurtful.—Venesection, Electricity, Epispastics, are nearly powerless as Anti-spasmodics. Valerian has been reckoned by many practitioners almost a specific in convulsion fits, but experience has proved that in nine cases out of ten it has been of no real service. Musk, Castor, Assafoetida, Peony Root, Viscus quercinum, Extractum hyosciami, and many other remedies, in which great confidence has been placed by the faculty, have been used without success. A medical gentleman of the present day has, however, discovered, after much study and labour, a remedy for this disorder, which is, in most cases, an absolute specific; and in the course of his extensive practice in one of the principal county towns in this Kingdom, he uses it with complete and unvarying success. To extend however so happy a discovery beyond the circuit of his immediate private practice, he has allowed it to be advertised, for the use of those afflicted with epileptic and convulsion fits, and the dreadful effects of those disorders. Printed directions for the use accompany each box, the price of which is 4s. 6d. duty included.

The Epilepsy often attacks suddenly, and without giving any warning; but is more frequently preceded by a pain in the head, lassitude, some disturbance of the senses, unquiet sleep, unusual dread; dimness of sight, a noise in the ears, palpitation of the heart, coldness of the joints, and in some there is a sensation of formication, or of cold air, &c. ascending from the lower extremities towards the head. In the fit, the patients fall suddenly to the ground (whence the name of the falling sickness) frequently with a violent cry.—The thumbs are shut up close in the palms of the hands, and are with difficulty [...]; the eyes are distorted, so that nothing but the whites are to be seen; all sensation is suspended, insomuch that by no noise, or otherwise, not even by pinching the body, can they be brought to themselves; they froth at the mouth, with a hissing kind of noise; the tongue is frequently lacerated by the teeth, and there is a violent convulsive motion of the arms and legs. Sometimes, however, the limbs, instead of being agitated by convulsive motions, are all stiff, and the patients are as immoveable as a statue. At length there is a remission of the symptoms, and the patients recover after a longer or shorter interval; when they complain of a pain, torpor, or heaviness of the head, with a lassitude of all the joints.

The disease will attack strong as well as weak people; and in those who have been subject to it, any considerable excess of drinking, violent passions, &c. will in general bring on a fit. Some have epileptic paroxysms returning periodically after considerable intervals; and the disease has been thought to have some dependence on the phases of the moon.—Vide the Edinburgh Practice of Physic and Surgery.) When the epilepsy attacks persons about their 21st year, and the fits continue to grow more frequent, the animal functions are often destroyed as well as those of the mind, and the patient becomes helpless and foolish. Sometimes it will terminate in melancholy or madness, and sometimes in a mortal apoplexy or palsy.

To guard against these dreadful consequences is a duty which the public owe to their afflicted neighbours, by administering to them Dr. Taylor's Anti-spasmodic Pills.

Sold wholesale by Barclay and Son, 95, Fleet-Market; and all the principal wholesale venders; retail by Matthews and Leigh [...]

The importance of local issues in Cornish politics was also reflected in the foundation in 1950 of Mebyon Kernow (Sons of Cornwall, in the Cornish language). This party, modelled on Plaid Cymru (Party of Wales) and the Scottish National Party, argued that Cornwall should have its own Assembly or Parliament, similar to those that have now been opened in Wales, Scotland and Northern Ireland. Although Mebyon Kernow candidates have never been elected to the House of Commons, some MK members have won seats on the County, District, Town and Parish Councils.

Local issues were also behind the rise of the 'Independent' tradition in Cornish politics. When the Local Government Act of 1888 created modern County Councils, all the candidates in the Cornish elections stood as Independents. Today, there are still many Independent councillors on both County and District Councils in Cornwall, despite the increasing intervention of the London-based parties and the virtual disappearance of the Independent tradition elsewhere in Britain.

Since 1888, local government in Britain has experienced several shake-ups. Although the boundaries of many counties have been altered, Cornwall has retained the River Tamar as its border. Similarly, in the Local Government Review of 1994-95, Cornwall emerged intact, with its two-tier system of County and District Councils surviving at a time when many counties were being split up.

Some people had argued that Cornwall should become a 'single unitary authority', in which the Districts would disappear and all principal local government powers would be given to the County Council, but by the late 1990s the argument had switched to the type of regional government best suited to Cornwall. As plans emerged for Regional Assemblies in the different parts of Britain, so people began to debate whether Cornwall would be better off in a large South West region or as a region in its own right.

This debate was echoed in discussions about Cornwall's place in Europe. The introduction of a large South West Constituency, in which Members of the European Parliament were elected by a new proportional representation method, put paid to the long-cherished hope that one day Cornwall might have its own seat in the European Parliament in Strasbourg. In 1998, however, the European Parliament recognised Cornwall as a region for economic planning purposes, a pointer perhaps to the way in which Cornish politics and power might develop in the twenty-first century.

The much-loved **David Penhaligon,** Liberal **MP for Truro from 1974** until his tragic death in a car accident in December 1986. His memorial service was listened to on **BBC Radio Cornwall** by an estimated 100,000 people. He is shown here in characteristic pose, sampling Cornish cream.

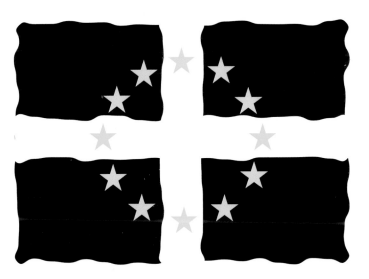

Penzance welcomes you

PENSANS
AS DYNERGH

Morgan Lowndes

language & literature

'In Cornwall is two speches;
the one is naughty Englyshe,
and the other Cornyshe speche.
And there may be many men
and women the which cannot
speake one word of Englyshe,
but all Cornyshe'

ANDREW BORDE
BOOK OF KNOWLEDGE
1542

In Cornwall there are two languages. English is the language of everyday communication, the language you will hear on the street, in the bus, at school or in college. But if you are lucky and if you listen carefully, you might also hear Cornish, the old language of Cornwall which almost died two hundred years ago.

Davies Gilbert was a Cornish politician and historian who lived from 1767 to 1839. He was fascinated by the language that in his lifetime seemed to be disappearing. He wrote a poem, arranged in alternate rhyme, using placenames to illustrate the haunting beauty of the Cornish language:

Today, more and more people are learning Cornish, and some are teaching it to their children in the home. If you look carefully, you will find that the Cornish language is all around us, not only in placenames and surnames but in the many new situations where Cornish is now in use. Many cars, for example, sport KERNOW stickers on their bumpers, Kernow being the Cornish language word for Cornwall.

Cornish was spoken here before the arrival of English. It is a member of the Celtic group of languages, very close to **Breton** and similar to **Welsh**, and less closely related to **Irish**, **Manx** and **Scots Gaelic**. People from 'up country' sometimes find Cornish names hard to say, but Cornish is an attractive language with a musical lilt all of its own.

Stablehobba Balaswhidden,

Tringey Trannack Try Trenear,

Fraddam Crowles Gwallan Crankan,

Drift Bojedna Cayle Trebear.

Haltergantic Carnaliezy,

Gumford Brunion Nancekeage,

Reen Trevasken Mevagizzy,

Killiow Carbus Carn Tretheage.

Placename spellings
may have changed a bit since Gilbert's day but
Cornish is no less enchanting for that.

onen 1 deu 2 try 3 peswar 4 pymp 5

Hic incipit ordinale de vita beati
meriadoci epi et confessor

6 whegh **7** seyth **8** eth **9** naw **10** dek

Cornish Numbers bear a striking similarity to Welsh and other Celtic tongues

There is also a substantial literature in the Cornish language, much of it dating from the Middle Ages when a series of lengthy miracle plays was written on a variety of religious themes. Although these plays have much in common with similar religious miracle plays written elsewhere in Europe at the time, they have many distinctly Cornish character-istics, and the fact that they are in the Cornish language makes them unique.

The earliest surviving play is the *Ordinalia*, dating from the fourteenth century, while *Beunans Meriasek* (the Life of St Meriasek) was written about 1500. Another play, *Gwreans an Bys* (the Creation of the World), was composed around 1530-40 but was copied out afresh by one William Jordan in Helston in 1611, an indication that the plays were still considered important even at that relatively late date.

However, the plays (which were Catholic in theme) and the Cornish language had already been dealt a severe blow by the introduction of the Protestant religion and the English Prayer Book in the 1500s. Thereafter, Cornish was in decline.

Piran Round, near Perranporth, dating from around 1400, where Cornish-language miracle plays were once performed.

A page from the surviving manuscript of the miracle play Beunans Meriasek (the Life of St Meriasek), written about 1500. The language is Cornish but the old-fashioned handwriting makes it very hard to read.

William Borlase produced these drawings as part of his *Natural History of Cornwall* in 1758. He travelled throughout Cornwall making drawings of ancient monuments and sites.

G   E   D   C

Plan of

B C D E F G

Round.

⁵⁰ 6̄0 7̄0

An 'aerial view' drawing by
Borlase of **Piran Round**
near Goonhavern. This is a
wonderful example of a
Plen-an-Gwarry or Playing
Place. The Miracle Plays
including **The Ordinalia**
were performed here and
at other rounds such as the
one at St Just in Penwith.

Although pockets of Cornish speakers survived in isolated areas of mid-Cornwall, it was in the west that the language survived longest.

When Edward Lhuyd, the Oxford scholar who undertook an extensive study of the Celtic languages, visited Cornwall in 1700 he found that Cornish was still spoken in some twenty-five parishes from Land's End to the Lizard. He also recorded an intriguing rhyme given to him by the parish clerk of St Just-in-Penwith:

An lavar koth yw lavar gwir,
> *The old saying is a true saying,*
Na boz nevra doz vaz an tavaz re hir;
> *A tongue too long never did good;*
Bez den heb davaz a gollaz i dir.
> *But the man with no tongue lost his land.*

Dolly Pentreath, the old Mousehole fishwife who died in 1777, is often said to have been the last person to have spoken Cornish. But we know that she was survived by other Cornish speakers, such as William Bodinar who died in 1789, and John Davey of Boswednack (near Zennor) who died in 1891 and was also thought to have known some Cornish.

Born in 1848 at
St Colomb Major,
Henry Jenner is
regarded as 'The Father
of the Cornish Revival'.
He was in fact of
Scottish and English
parentage. As Robert
Morton Nance once
wrote, it was open to
Jenner 'to choose any of
three nationalities.
He chose from the first
to be Cornish'. Jenner's
*A Handbook of Cornish
Language* was published
in 1904.

Drew goz hanaw?
What is your name?

Jenifer henwez o ve.
My name is Jenifer.

Cornish counting rhymes survived amongst the fishermen at Newlyn perhaps even into the 1920s and 1930s, while many Cornish language words were absorbed into the Cornish dialect of English. By then, however, moves were already afoot to revive the Cornish language. Scholars such as Henry Jenner and Robert Morton Nance worked hard in the early decades of the twentieth century to reconstruct the language so that others might learn it, and soon dictionaries appeared and evening classes were established.

Today, there are three ways of spelling and pronouncing Cornish. These examples are in 'Modern' Cornish, based on the language as it was last spoken traditionally in Cornwall in the seventeenth and eighteenth centuries.

After the Second World War, the revival of the Cornish language became even more popular, and today organisations such as the Cornish Language Council, the Cornish Language Board and Agan Tavas ('Our Language') offer a wide range of facilities for those wishing to learn Cornish.

This enthusiasm for the Cornish language has meant that the Cornish dialect of English has sometimes been overlooked by those anxious to celebrate Cornish culture. However, Jack Clemo, the blind and deaf writer of the china clay country (who died in 1994), was one Cornish writer to use dialect effectively in his work. His dialect short stories, many published in the inter-War years, proved extremely popular.

But Clemo was best known as a poet, and it was his poetry that won him international acclaim. His gritty portrayal of the clay country around St Austell seemed to fit his austere religious views:

Jack Clemo
Many of Clemo's dialect stories appeared in the 1930s in annuals such as *Sunday Almanack*, published in Penzance, Truro's *Netherton's Almanack* and the *One and All Almanack* published at Camborne. They have a dry, pithy humour which is very Cornish:
'*Sammy Chegwidden had traipsed around Pengooth village four times that evening afore he catched sight of Maria Blake; and he wad'n much better off when he did see her*'.

Yes, I might well grow tired
Of slighting flowers all day long,
Of making my song
Of the mud in the kiln, of the wired
Poles of the clay dump...
Is there a flower that thrills
Like frayed rope? Is there grass
That cools like gravel, and are there streams
Which murmur as clay-silt does
— that Christ redeems?

D.M. Thomas is another contemporary writer, author and poet, who has drawn upon his Cornish background to give content and meaning to his work. So too is Charles Causley, the Launceston poet:

> My young man's a Cornishman
> He lives in Camborne town,
> I met him going up the hill
> As I was coming down.
>
> His eye is bright as Dolcoath tin,
> His body as china clay,
> His hair is dark as Werrington Wood
> Upon St Thomas's Day.

Other Cornish writers at work today include N.R. Phillips, whose novel *The Saffron Eaters* drew high praise, and Donald R. Rawe, the author, playwright and publisher. Donald Rawe's Lodenek Press, founded at Padstow, is one example of a very Cornish tradition, the growth of small publishing houses since the War (such as Dyllansow Truran, Tor Mark Press, Tabb House, Cornish Hillside, and Alexander Associates) dedicated to the publication of Cornish books written by local authors.

'BY TRE, POL, AND PEN YOU SHALL KNOW THE CORNISHMEN'

RICHARD CAREW

Richard Carew of Antony (near Torpoint) wrote the classic *Survey of Cornwall* in 1602. By the time he was writing, the Cornish miracle plays were falling into decline and disrepute. Carew described how the actors deliberately fluffed their lines and messed up their performances. But the audience did not mind: '*it defrauded not the beholders, but dismissed them with a great deal more sport and laughter than twenty such gwaries (miracle plays) could have afforded.*'

Of course, the writing of books in and about Cornwall is not new. In 1602 Richard Carew of Antony (near Torpoint) published his classic *Survey of Cornwall*, a book that even today is much loved and is still an important source of information about Cornwall. Later, in the nineteenth century, the Hocking brothers– Joseph and Silas– from St Stephen-in-Brannel– wrote Cornish novels inspired by their Methodist beliefs.

Sir Arthur Quiller Couch (or 'Q' as he came to be known in Cornish and literary circles) spent much of his life in Fowey, where he died in 1944, but he was also Professor of English at the University of Cambridge. He wrote poetry and novels, such as *The Splendid Spur* set in Cornwall in the Civil Wars. A.L.Rowse, the famous Cornish historian and Oxford scholar who died in 1997, also wrote short stories and poems, such as the one opposite: *Cornish Landscape*.

The National Trust

Sir Arthur Quiller Couch pictured as a young man in Fowey.

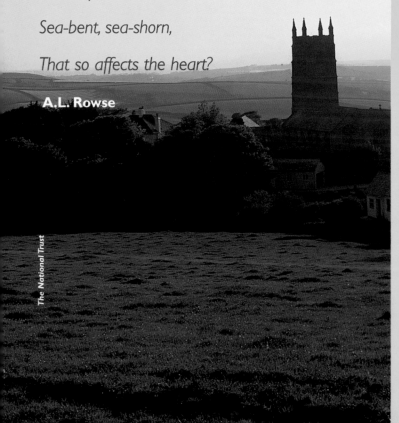

The rich red of evening sun on the harrowed field,

The chittering of birds,

The insistent drone of planes out to sea,

The scolding rooks,

The colder tones of the water:

What is there in a Cornish hedge,

The broken herring-bone pattern of stones,

The gorse, the ragged rick,

The way the little elms are,

Sea-bent, sea-shorn,

That so affects the heart?

A.L. Rowse

The National Trust

Dr A.L. Rowse,
born at Tregonissey, near
St Austell, in 1903, wrote
more than 100 books and
countless articles before
his death at Trenarren
(also near St Austell) in
1997. Amongst his most
famous books are *Tudor
Cornwall* and *A Cornish
Childhood*. The latter, first
published in 1942, tells
the struggle of his early
years, from humble
beginnings as the son of a
poor clayworker to his
successful quest to study
at the University of
Oxford. This photograph
was taken in 1927, a few
years after he had been
appointed Fellow of
All Souls, one of the
Oxford colleges.

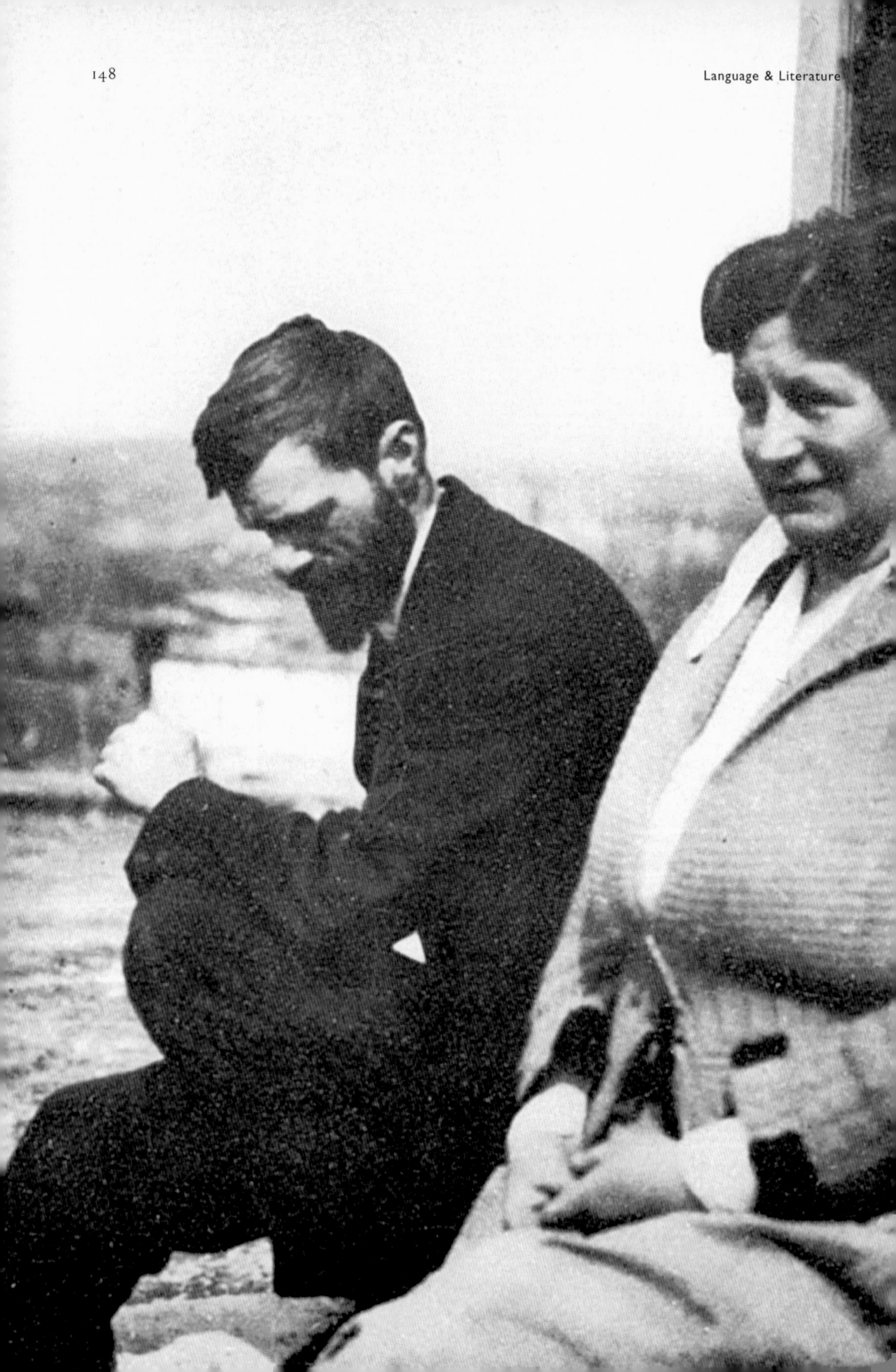

'O the opal and the sapphire of that wandering western sea'

In addition to all these Cornish writers, many 'foreign' authors have been attracted to Cornwall from across the Tamar. Thomas Hardy, who wrote the famous 'Wessex' novels about his native Dorset, also wrote *A Pair of Blue Eyes*, set in North Cornwall, together with a number of poems on Cornish themes. D.H. Lawrence spent time at Zennor during the First World War, using his experiences there to help write his book *Kangaroo*. Daphne du Maurier, who wrote a string of bestsellers set in Cornwall, among them *Rebecca* and *Jamaica Inn*, lived for many years at Menabilly, near Fowey. Winston Graham wrote the *Poldark* novels about Ross Poldark and Demelza, which were later adapted for television, and E.V. Thompson has written a series of novels based on nineteenth-century Cornwall, including his well-known *Chase The Wind*.

Thomas Hardy wrote the above lines in his famous poem *'Beeny Cliff'*, composed after a visit to Cornwall in 1912 following his wife's death.

D.H. Lawrence and his German-born wife Freida at Tregerthen, near Zennor, during the First World War. Freida was related to the German air force 'ace', the 'Red Baron' Von Richtofen. Worse still, Lawrence and Freida insisted on singing German songs at the top of their voices, and local people suggested they might be 'German spies', signalling secretly to enemy submarines lurking off the Cornish coast. In the end, the Lawrences were thrown out of Cornwall by the Government, a deeply upsetting experience which D.H. Lawrence explained in his book *Kangaroo*.

Made famous by Daphne du Maurier's novel of the same name, **Jamaica Inn** is a favourite stop-off point for motorists crossing Bodmin Moor.

Simon Cook

'Last night I dreamt I went to Manderley again...'

Daphne du Maurier *Rebecca*

Cornwall meets Hollywood. In 1940 Daphne du Maurier's best-selling book *Rebecca* was made into an internationally successful film by Alfred Hitchcock, starring the famous actors Joan Fontaine (left) and Laurence Olivier (centre), together with Judith Anderson (right) who played the scary Mrs Danvers.

EN ROUTE FOR NORTH CORNWALL

THE " LORD NELSON " WITH ATLANTIC COAST EXPRESS
LEAVING WATERLOO STATION FOR NORTH CORNWALL.

The one-time Poet Laureate, the late Sir John Betjeman, spent his childhood holidays in North Cornwall, at Trebetherick and Polzeath. He died here in 1984, and is buried in the churchyard at St Enodoc. His Cornish poems sum up somehow the sense of 'difference', of Cornwall as a land apart, that has continued to draw writers and artists from outside:

The emptying train, wind in the ventilators,

Puffs out of Egloskerry to Tresmeer

Through minty meadows, under bearded trees

And hills upon whose sides the clinging farms

Hold Bible Christians. Can it really be

That this same carriage came from Waterloo?

On Wadebridge station what a breath of sea

Scented the Camel valley! Cornish air,

Soft Cornish rains, and silence after steam . . .

As out of Derry's stable came the brake

To drag us up those long, familiar hills,

Past haunted woods and oil-lit farms and on

To far Trebetherick by the sounding sea.

John Betjeman was born in London in 1906 and died at Trebetherick in Cornwall in 1984. He fell in love with Cornwall during his childhood holidays on the north coast, and returned here almost every year until his death. He wrote about Cornwall in both poem and prose, and when he was away Cornwall was never far from his thoughts:

'St Protus and St Hyacinth, patron saints of Blisland church, pray for me! Often in a bus or train I call to mind your lovely church, the stillness of that Cornish valley and the first really beautiful work of man which my boyhood vividly remembers'.

Jane Bown

'The Cornish are remarkable for their sanguine temperament, their indomitable perseverance, their ardent hope in adventure, and their desire for discovery and novelty ... to this very cause has science to boast of so many brilliant ornaments who claim Cornwall as their birthplace'.

GEORGE HENWOOD
THE MINING JOURNAL
1859

Richard Trevithick
and **Nicholas Holman** with
their 40 foot long high pressure
steam boiler at **Camborne** in
1815, depicted in a painting by
Terence Cuneo.

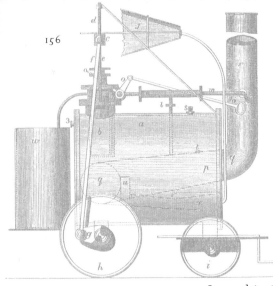

Richard Trevithick
was the first engineer in
the world to create a
road-going vehicle, in
effect the first 'car'.

Cornwall is the timeless land, a place of ancient landscapes and frequent echoes of the long-ago: burial chambers, standing stones, Celtic crosses, holy wells. But Cornwall is also the home of modernity, its history peppered with Cornish achievements from Richard Trevithick's invention of the railway locomotive to the array of high-tech businesses active here at the beginning of the third Millennium.

Legend insists that Cornwall was trading its tin with the Phoenicians before the coming of the Romans, a glimpse of the international role the Cornish were to play centuries later in Britain's Industrial Revolution. Mining techniques, including the application of water power, developed apace in Cornwall during the Middle Ages and the Early Modern period. When steam was harnessed in the cause of industrialisation, the Cornish were amongst the first to exploit its possibilities.

Inside the great foundry of Harvey & Co. of Hayle, where Cornish engines, boilers and all manner of state-of-the-art mining machinery was made for destinations the world over.

As early as 1716 there was a Newcomen steam engine working as a pump in a Cornish mine, probably at Great Wheal Vor or at neighbouring Godolphin Ball (both near Helston), while by the 1770s the more economical Watt engines were in use in Cornwall. When James Watt's patents lapsed in 1800, allowing Cornish engineers to install their own improved designs, Cornwall became even more important as a home of steam engine development. The 'Cornish engine', with its characteristic rocking beam or 'bob' and the tall castle-like structure in which it was housed, soon became a familiar feature of the Cornish landscape.

Foundries sprang up across Cornwall to build Cornish engines and all manner of other machinery for mines at home and abroad. Among the most famous were Harvey's of Hayle, the Perran Foundry at Perranarworthal, and William West of St Blazey.

Royal Institution of Cornwall

In the 1840s **Harvey & Co.** of Hayle was asked by the Dutch government to manufacture giant pumping engines to drain Haarlem Meer, part of a project to reclaim land from the sea and protect Holland from drowning. These engines had huge cylinders of 84 inches and 144 inches cast in iron, weighing up to 25 tons. One of the cylinders was found, after casting, to be faulty and was placed on the road opposite the foundry, a favourite place for dramatic photographs in subsequent years

Miners riding the man engine at **Dolcoath Mine**, Camborne, a photograph taken by J.C. Burrow in about 1893 'at the 234 fathom level below adit'.

Cornish engines were used for pumping water from the ever deeper tin and copper mines. They were also used to operate 'stamps' (machinery for crushing ore) and as winding or 'whim' engines to haul to surface the ore mined in the dark 'stopes' far below ground. The miners themselves had to climb up and down the shafts by a series of ladders, a tiring and dangerous activity, although at some mines a 'man-engine' was introduced. This consisted of a huge rod of joined timbers, driven by a Cornish beam engine, which moved alternately up and down in the shaft. Steps were attached to the rod, and to ascend or descend the miner stepped on or off at each stage or 'level' until he had reached the top or bottom.

Miners enjoying their 'Crowst' or 'Crib' (a snack, usually a pasty) at East Pool Mine, between Camborne and Redruth, about 1893.

Group of Cornish Miners at the bottom of the shaft at King Edward Mine, Camborne, about 1893.

Relatives of miners at Levant Mine wait anxiously for news of their loved ones at the time of the disaster on the 20th October 1919.

In 1919 there was a terrible accident at the Levant mine, near St Just-in-Penwith, when the man-engine rod broke, killing some 31 miners. Another disaster was the flooding of East Wheal Rose mine, at Newlyn East, after a freak rain storm on 5 July 1846, when thirty-nine miners lost their lives. There are numerous other stories of accidents in Cornish mines. Rock falls underground were a common cause of injury and death, and so too were premature explosions (when miners were blasting the rock) and the many cases of exhausted miners 'falling away' from ladders. There were also boiler explosions, and sometimes mine-workers were horribly maimed when accidentally caught up in moving machinery.

The men and boys working underground were those most likely to be hurt in mining accidents but sometimes the women and girls employed at surface to sort and grade the ore were also injured or killed: perhaps by becoming entangled in machinery, or falling down an unguarded shaft. These women and girls, or 'bal-maidens' as they were known (after the Cornish language word 'bal', a mine), were a familiar part of the Cornish mining scene until machinery took over their role in the latter part of the nineteenth century.

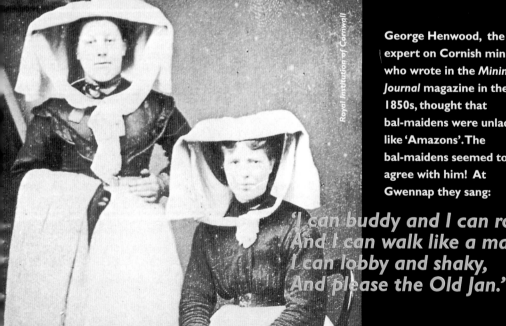

Royal Institution of Cornwall

George Henwood, the expert on Cornish mining who wrote in the *Mining Journal* magazine in the 1850s, thought that bal-maidens were unlady-like 'Amazons'. The bal-maidens seemed to agree with him! At Gwennap they sang:

*'I can buddy and I can rocky.
And I can walk like a man,
I can lobby and shaky,
And please the Old Jan.'*

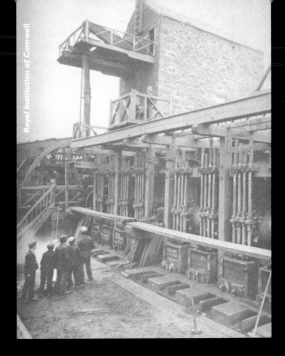

Steam driven stamps for crushing ore at the **Levant Mine**, near St Just-in-Penwith in 1910.

PENPOLL TIN SMELTING Cº LTD TRURO

An example of the dies used by **Cornish** smelting works to stamp their ingots or bars of smelted tin.

A cross-section along the Main Lode at **Dolcoath Mine**, Camborne, around 1900.

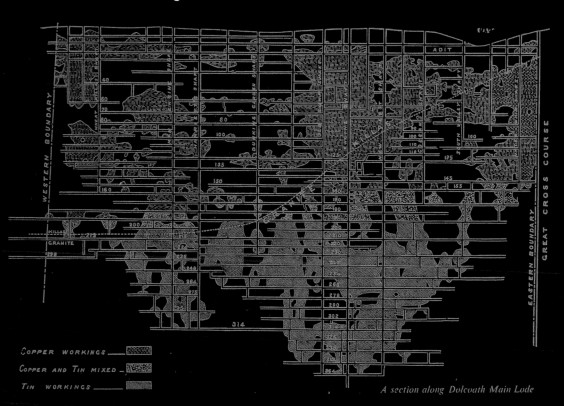

COPPER WORKINGS
COPPER AND TIN MIXED
TIN WORKINGS

A section along Dolcoath Main Lode

Tin had been streamed and mined in Cornwall since ancient times but it was copper that accounted for the great boom in Cornish mining in the eighteenth and nineteenth centuries. The parish of Gwennap, with famous mines such as Wheal Fortune, Ting Tang, and Wheal Maid, was known in those days as 'the richest square mile on earth'. The district around Camborne and Redruth was also part of the heartland of Cornish copper, but from about 1810 onwards copper mining began to expand to other parts of Cornwall. In the far west St Just-in-Penwith emerged as an important copper mining district, and so too did the St Austell area of mid-Cornwall.

In 1836 copper was found at Caradon Hill, near Liskeard, and soon the parishes of St Cleer and Linkinhorne were full of mines and miners. Lead was found in the neighbouring parish of Menheniot and further south at Herodsfoot, while there were further strikes of copper in the Tamar valley around Callington, Calstock, Gunnislake and across the Devon border at Tavistock.

Alongside this expansion of copper, tin continued to be worked across Cornwall, with areas such as Marazion, Breage and Wendron emerging as important tin producers. Before long, every part of Cornwall seemed to have its Cornish mines – including such far-flung workings as Wheal Carew at Torpoint, Wheal Tamar at Saltash, and Wheal Morwenna at Morwenstow.

The mighty engine house at East Wheal Rose silver-lead mine, near St Newlyn East, long after it was abandoned but before it was restored.

Mining took place in most areas of Cornwall, as this map indicates.

Some mines in Cornwall were incredibly deep. This illustration compares Cornwall's deepest mine at Dolcoath with world famous tall buildings.

Illustration by Blade McGivern, BA (Hons) Illustration, Falmouth College of Arts

| St Paul's Cathedral | The Great Pyramid at Giza | Eiffel Tower | The Bank of China | Empire State | Dolcoath Mine |

Mike Newman

After the crash of Cornish copper in 1866 many of the big Camborne and Redruth mines, such as Dolcoath, luckily struck tin at depth and were able to continue working. A short-lived tin boom in the early 1870s was followed by deep depression as overseas producers forced down the price of tin. Since then, the story of Cornish tin mining has been one of continual decline, punctuated occasionally by new bursts of optimism and renewed activity.

In the 1970s and 1980s the industry seemed to be enjoying a comeback, with tin mines in production at Geevor, Wheal Jane, Mount Wellington, Wheal Concord, Wheal Pendarves, and South Crofty. By the mid-1990s only South Crofty remained, the last tin mine in Europe, but even it fell victim to low tin prices and overseas competition, and was closed in 1998.

Tin mining was survived by that other great Cornish extractive industry, china clay. Discovered in Cornwall in 1746 by the Plymouth chemist, William Cookworthy, china clay was quarried in various locations from St Just-in-Penwith to Bodmin Moor. The Hensbarrow uplands north of St Austell, however, have become the heart of Cornwall's 'china clay country', with villages such as Treviscoe, Bugle, Foxhole, Stenalees, Nanpean, St Dennis and St Stephen-in-Brannel seemingly dominated by this vast industry.

Today, there are fewer people employed in the china clay industry than before, while parts of the distinctively white 'lunar landscape' have been reclaimed and returned to Nature. But china clay still provides an important contribution to the Cornish economy.

Other extractive industries have included the quarrying of slate at Delabole and St Neot, and of granite at Constantine, Mabe, St Breward, Cheesewring and other sites throughout Cornwall.

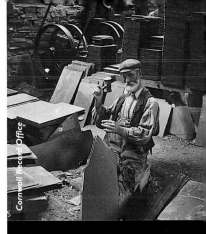

Cornwall Record Office

The highly skilled art of splitting Cornish slates at Delabole in the 1920s.

The stark landscape of a China Clay pit, near St Austell.

Paul Watts

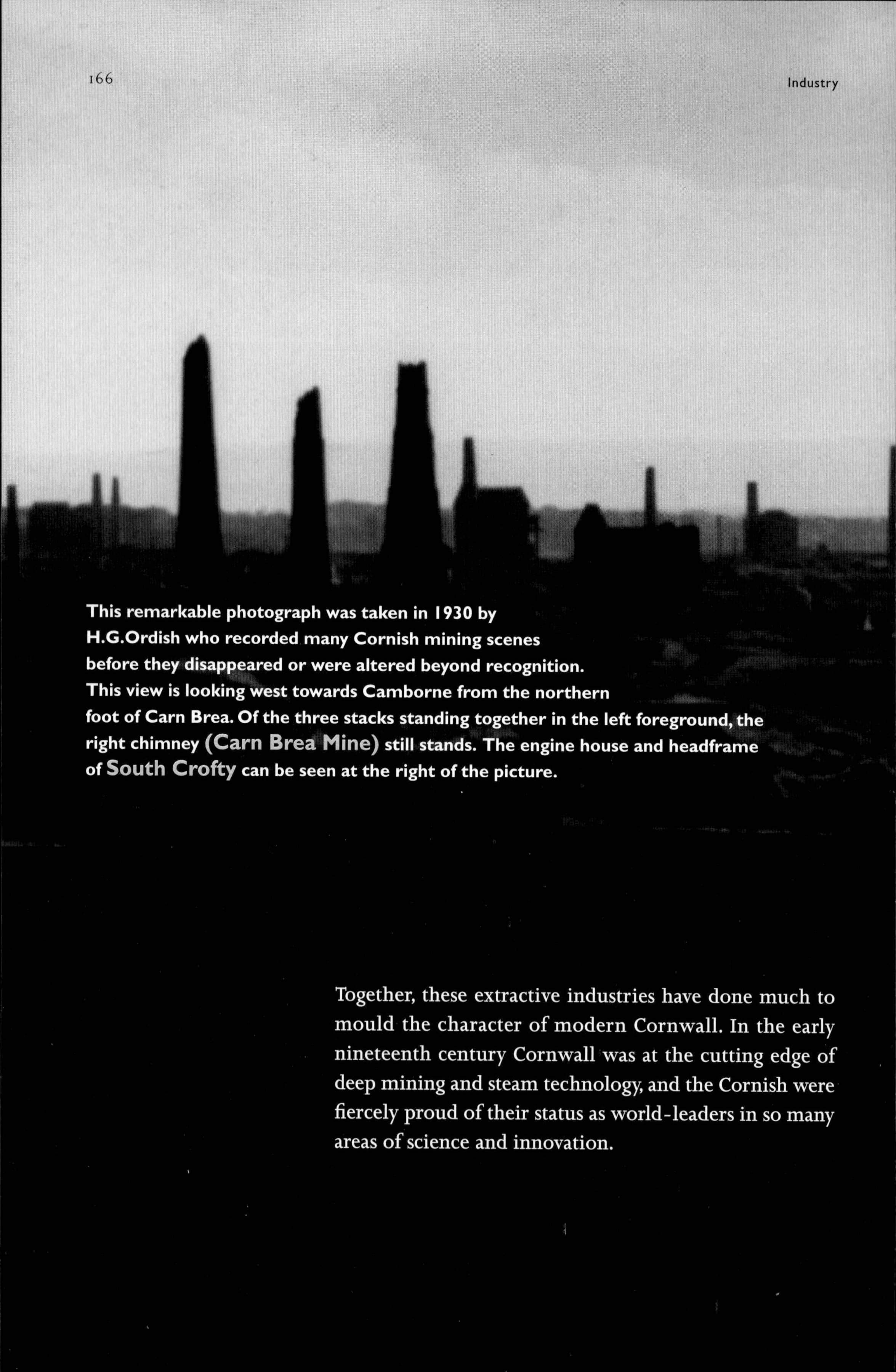

This remarkable photograph was taken in 1930 by
H.G.Ordish who recorded many Cornish mining scenes
before they disappeared or were altered beyond recognition.
This view is looking west towards Camborne from the northern
foot of Carn Brea. Of the three stacks standing together in the left foreground, the
right chimney (Carn Brea Mine) still stands. The engine house and headframe
of South Crofty can be seen at the right of the picture.

Together, these extractive industries have done much to
mould the character of modern Cornwall. In the early
nineteenth century Cornwall was at the cutting edge of
deep mining and steam technology, and the Cornish were
fiercely proud of their status as world-leaders in so many
areas of science and innovation.

1930

However, the rapid decline of copper and then tin mining in the latter part of the nineteenth century did much to knock Cornish self-confidence and called into question this identity based on industrial prowess. This was one reason why some Cornish people in the early twentieth century turned to the so-called 'Celtic Revival' for new ideas about the future of Cornwall.

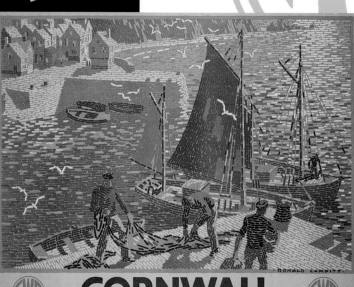

These people thought that, by looking back to an earlier Celtic era before the Industrial Revolution, they could build a new 'post-industrial' Cornwall. They planned the revival of the Cornish language but they also encouraged discussion about the development of tourism. Some saw tourism as the means of filling the economic gap left by the decline of mining, while others argued that the image of Cornwall as a Celtic 'land of difference' would be very attractive to potential tourists. This idea was taken up enthusiastically by the Great Western Railway, which cleverly included Celtic legends and Celtic sites (such as crosses and holy wells) in its literature advertising the 'Cornish Riviera'.

Great Western Railway posters from the early 1930s used evocative images of Cornwall to attract visitors. In the example below by Ronald Lampitt, a mosaic style has been used to illustrate a Cornish fishing village.

1936

CORNWALL

The railways played a major role in developing mass tourism in Cornwall, particularly in the inter-war years between 1918 and 1939. After 1945, tourists in large numbers returned once again to Cornwall, initially by train but – by the 1960s – increasingly by car. Tourism was by then established as a major Cornish 'industry', although by the 1970s and 1980s critics were emerging. Some thought that too many tourists were coming to Cornwall, spoiling those very things that had attracted people in the first place, while others argued that the thousands of people enticed to Cornwall by promises of 'sea, sand and sunshine' would sooner or later switch their attentions to overseas destinations (such as Spain) where good weather could be guaranteed.

By the 1990s, therefore, the tourist industry was increasingly trying to attract a new type of visitor, one who would come to Cornwall in search of 'heritage'. In the forefront of this new heritage tourism was the lavish attention given to old mining sites. Only recently shunned as dangerous and unattractive wastelands, the old mining areas of Cornwall were now seen as precious areas which could be highly attractive to tourists from the UK and abroad. The Great Flat Lode, the mining landscape to the south of Carn Brea in the Camborne-Redruth district, was nominated by the government in 1999 as the major part of a potential Cornish 'World Heritage Site', such was its new significance.

Surfing is not that new – as can be seen from this picture, taken in the early 1930s.

Many **Guide books** such as the Ward Lock series were produced in the 1920s to help tourists find their way around Cornwall.

The Great Flat Lode, south of Carn Brea, seen from the air.

East Pool Engine at Pool, between Redruth and Camborne, now in the care of the Trevithick Trust.

The National Trust

Cornwall Archeological Unit

All pictures courtesy of 'In Pursuit of Excellence' and Creative Edge, Truro

Falmouth **continues to win major ship repair contracts and provides a significant number of skilled jobs.**

The changing nature of tourism was reflected in other changes in the Cornish economy. Despite the decline of mining, the industrial spirit had not disappeared. As well as the survival of china clay, ship-repairing and other long-established industries, a new generation of precision, micro-engineering and other small businesses had emerged by the 1990s. Set alongside developments in communications and information technology, this seemed to point the way ahead for Cornish manufacturing and perhaps for the Cornish economy as a whole. The *In Pursuit of Excellence* initiative, designed to draw international attention to a range of high-quality products from Cornwall, chronicled the activities of new companies such as Gul (manufacturers of wet-suits) and of successful Cornish firms such as GeoScience and Radio-Code Ltd, Seacore and Maybridge Chemicals, all of which regularly exported their products across the Tamar.

The Zenky Beam Seating system is designed and manufactured by Zoeftig and Company in Bude, and used in locations all over the world.

Pendennis Shipyard,
based in **Falmouth Docks**, export
90% of the Superyachts their expert
workforce build and refurbish.

Richard Mozley
invented this machine
to remove fine solids
from fluids. The company
now exports half of all
the equipment it
manufactures at its
factory in Redruth.

Gul International,
based in **Bodmin**, is
one of the world's
best known wetsuit
manufacturers.

the great emigration

'Wherever
in the
World
there's a
hole in
the
ground
at the
bottom
of it
you'll
find a
Cornishman
searching
for metal'

A.K. HAMILTON JENKIN
THE CORNISH MINER
1927

The engine house illustrated here is NOT in Cornwall – if you look closely you will soon see the sombreros! It is actually a mine in Mexico in about 1880.

1846

Cousin Jack was an often used nickname for a Cornish miner; today it is still used all over the world to describe Cornish men. Cornish women, of course, are Cousin Jennies.

Cornish farmers at Helston Farm, Dunsandel, near Christchurch, Canterbury, New Zealand. Not all Cornish emigrants were miners.

'Wherever in the World there's a hole in the ground at the bottom of it you'll find a Cornishman searching for metal'. Even today this is true enough, but in the nineteenth century – the era of Cornwall's 'Great Emigration' – this saying was a sobering fact of life for thousands of Cornish families whose menfolk toiled in mines the world over, from Peru and Bolivia to Tasmania and New Zealand.

But it was only part of the story, for in addition to the men (the 'Cousin Jacks' as they were known) thousands of women or 'Cousin Jennies' also made their way to far-flung mining districts such as Grass Valley in California and Moonta in South Australia. Moreover, many of those who left Cornwall for overseas destinations were not miners, their occupations ranging from farmers and agricultural labourers to female domestic servants and housewives.

Although the Cornish were already well-known for their exploits across the globe as navigators and explorers, it was not until the end of the Napoleonic Wars in 1815 that large numbers of people began to consider leaving Cornwall to start new lives in new countries overseas.

After 1815, many Cornish people in agricultural areas such as North Cornwall and the Lizard complained about high taxes and high rents. Many were Methodists and objected to paying tithes – a proportion of their income – to the Church of England, a church to which they felt they did not belong.

EMIGRATION

TO

South Australia,

Mr. I. Latimer,

(AGENT FOR SOUTH AUSTRALIA)

Having been requested to explain the principles of COLONIZATION adopted by the SOUTH AUSTRALIAN COMMISSIONERS with regard to this Colony, begs to announce that he will deliver

A FREE

LECTURE

ON TUESDAY EVENING NEXT, AUGUST 27, 1839,

At the King's Head Inn, Chacewater.

As the Lecture is particularly intended for the instruction and benefit of the WORKING CLASSES, it is hoped that all those who feel interested in the subject will give their attendance punctually.

The Lecture will commence at Seven o'clock *precisely*, and at the conclusion the Lecturer will be happy to answer any questions relative to the Colony. Mr. Latimer will be in attendance at the KING'S HEAD previously, to give information to any Laborer, Mechanic, or Artisan, who may be desirous of obtaining a FREE PASSAGE to the Colony.

Truro, August 19, 1839.

E. HEARD, PRINTER, &c., BOSCAWEN-STREET, TRURO.

By the 1840s, when the potato blight hit Cornwall as it did Ireland and the Highlands of Scotland, thousands of hungry Cornish folk clamoured to escape starvation by going overseas. In subsequent decades, they were followed by thousands more. This group is about to board ship at Plymouth in 1870.

1870

This is the emigrant ship **Empress of China**, built at Padstow, which took hundreds of Cornish emigrants to Australia before she was wrecked off Tasmania in 1888.

When opportunities arose to emigrate to Canada or the United States of America, many of these Methodist farming families left Cornwall to journey to newly opened-up agricultural country in areas such as Wisconsin and Ontario. Whole families went out, taking advantage of the cheap fares that were available, and Padstow became a major port for this 'emigration trade'. Many Cornish people felt that they were exchanging the land of bondage (Britain) for the lands of the free (the United States or Canada).

At the same time, British businesses became interested in Latin America. The local colonial powers, Spain and Portugal, were in the process of being ejected from their American possessions and British companies thought that this might create opportunities for them to make money. With this in mind, British mining companies worked hard to develop the silver, gold and copper deposits of newly-independent Latin America, recruiting Cornish miners to travel to Mexico, Brazil, Cuba, Bolivia, Chile, Colombia and Venezuela. Although some Cornish miners took their families with them, many others went alone, sending 'homepay' (part of their earnings) back to Cornwall to support their wives, children and parents.

This is what many were searching for...

LEAD

GOLD

By the 1840s, when the potato blight hit Cornwall as it did Ireland and the Highlands of Scotland, thousands of hungry Cornish folk clamoured to escape starvation by going overseas. By then lead had already been found in Wisconsin, while the discovery of copper on the Great Lakes in America and at Burra Burra and Kapunda in South Australia had created important new destinations for Cornish emigrants. British colonies such as South Australia and New South Wales operated free and assisted passage schemes for intending emigrants, a further incentive for the poor or discontented in Cornwall to venture abroad.

Cornish miners at the New Almaden quicksilver (or mercury) mine in California.

In 1848 gold was discovered in California, and soon the Cornish influx began – from Cornwall itself but also from Cornish mining communities in Mexico and Australia. Along the Mother Lode country (so called because of its vast reserves of gold) of California and in the high mountains of the Sierra Nevada, the Cousin Jacks and Jennies made their mark. Later, several of the Californian Cornish travelled on to Australia, where in 1851 they joined the gold rush in Victoria which put such places as Ballarat and Bendigo on the international Cornish mining map.

EMIGRATION
TO
SOUTH
AUSTRALIA

Her Majesty's Colonization Commissioners having determined to dispatch in the course of a few weeks a large number of Emigrants, all eligible persons may obtain, by making an IMMEDIATE application, a

FREE
PASSAGE!

The classes of persons now in requisition are
Agricultural Laborers,
SHEPHERDS, CARPENTERS
BLACKSMITHS
AND
STONE MASONS
And all Persons connected with Building.
Application to be made to

Mr. I. LATIMER,
Rosewin-row, TRURO.

SILVER   TIN   COPPER

The Cornish Abroad. Highly skilled Cornish miners were much in demand in the rapidly developing international mining economy in the 19th century. These miners and their families created their own 'Little Cornwall' Cornish communities in countries all over the globe.

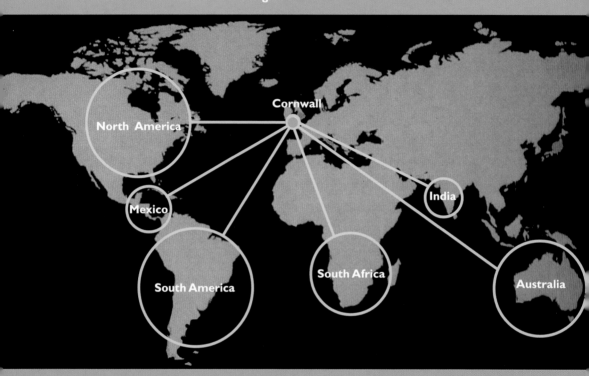

The houses below look like many in villages across Cornwall. In fact they were built at Mineral Point, Wisconsin, in the United States of America.

Cornish miners descend the deep shaft at the start of a long day at the Empire Mine in Grass Valley, California. This picture was taken around 1890.

Greetings from Callington in Australia!

Elder's pump engine at Wallaroo Mines, South Australia in 1887, built originally by Harveys & Co. of Hayle.

Moonta Mines in South Australia, the heart of 'Australia's Little Cornwall', in 1897. The large engine house in the background contains a 60 inch Cornish pumping engine built by Harvey & Co. of Hayle in 1863.

In 1859 copper was discovered at Wallaroo, back in South Australia, to be followed by an equally spectacular find at neighbouring Moonta. This region, South Australia's Yorke Peninsula, was soon dubbed 'Australia's Little Cornwall' – and no wonder, given the importance there of Cornish people, technology and culture. Mining machinery had been brought out directly from Cornwall, as had Cornish Methodism, Cornish wrestling, Cornish carols, brass bands, saffron cake, pasties, and numerous other Cornish customs. Together, the district of Moonta, Wallaroo and Kadina was probably the largest concentration of Cornish people outside Cornwall itself.

The 1860s were hard times for Cornwall, and in 1866 the bottom fell out of the Cornish copper mining industry. Almost overnight, scores of Cornish mines were abandoned, their miners thrown out of work. By then, however, the Cornish were already used to emigrating across the world in search of work, and after 1866 many more people left Cornwall to join the Cornish communities already established in North America and Australasia. Cousin Jacks and Cousin Jennies tended to stick together in these new countries, with newcomers from Cornwall welcomed with promises of jobs and lodgings.

Cousin Jacks underground, at Wallaroo Mines, South Australia.

Burra Burra Mine, South Australia, painted by ST Gill in 1850.

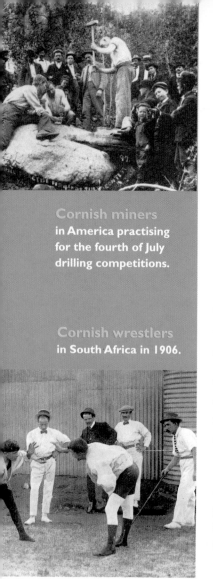

Cornish miners in America practising for the fourth of July drilling competitions.

Cornish wrestlers in South Africa in 1906.

The Cornish also argued that they were the most skilled miners in the world, and persuaded mine owners the world over to give them employment preference when confronted with competing groups such as the Irish, Italians, Finns and Croats. Many people were jealous of the status and privileges of the Cousin Jacks, and sometimes bad feeling spilled over into violence and conflict. But at other times the various ethnic groups lived and worked together harmoniously, sharing each other's customs and attending each other's celebrations.

The Cornish might march in St Patrick's Days parades, while the Irish might participate in Cornish wrestling and rock-drilling competitions.

On the new mining frontier of America, the Cornish established themselves in mining towns such as Virginia City in Nevada, Butte in Montana, and Leadville, Colorado, competing with the Irish for dominance in the mines and in

The platform at Redruth railway station in the early twentieth century thronged with Cornish on their way to Southampton to join ships bound for South Africa.

public life. In Australia the Cornish also emerged as a dominant group in the social, economic, cultural and political life of Broken Hill (New South Wales) in the 1880s and Kalgoorlie (Western Australia) in the 1890s.

By then important new mineral discoveries in South Africa had caught the attention of Cornwall. The diamond fields of Kimberley and, more especially, the gold fields of the Transvaal proved important magnets for the Cornish in the years before and after the turn of the twentieth century. Some served in the British forces in the Zulu and Boer wars but most of the Cornish were miners, many travelling to and fro' between Cornwall and South Africa.

Improved communications (including the introduction of steam ships) had by then made travel between Cornwall and South Africa (or America) relatively easy, and for this reason the closing years of the nineteenth century saw fewer families leaving Cornwall as permanent colonists but many more (often single men) leaving for temporary sojourns overseas.

In this way, many Cornish towns and villages were left in the control of women, with wives, mothers, sisters, daughters acting as heads of households in the often extended absences of the men.

Cornish Schoolchildren at Kooringa, near the Burra Burra copper mine, in South Australia.

The Union Castle liner **Arndale Castle** which carried many Cornish miners between Southampton and Cape Town during the early twentieth century.

A gravestone memorial far from home to 'John George', son of Cornwall.

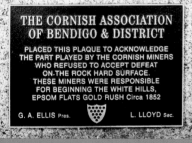

A plaque erected by the Cornish enthusiasts of Bendigo, Victoria, Australia, in the 1990's.

The crash of Cornish copper was followed in the 1870s by the faltering of Cornish tin, and still further mines were abandoned. But Cornish miners in South Africa were earning good money, and by the outbreak of the First World War in 1914 the well-being of many Cornish communities such as St Just-in-Penwith, Lanner, St Day, St Cleer and Gunnislake was dependent on financial support sent home from overseas.

However, after the end of the war in 1918, there were fewer jobs available in South Africa. Many came home to find that Cornwall was in the grip of an economic depression, with high unemployment and poor prospects. To make matters worse, many had developed 'miner's complaint' in South Africa, lung disease caused by the fine quartz dust when digging for gold. During the 1920s many Cousin Jacks came home from South Africa to suffer an early death due to 'miner's complaint'.

By the 1920s opportunities to emigrate abroad had almost disappeared, although the government offered assistance for unemployed Cornish miners travelling to the Hollinger gold mines in Ontario, while still others made their way to the great automobile manufacturing city of Detroit (Michigan) or to Grass Valley (California). To all intents and purposes, however, the 'Great Emigration' was over.

In all, as many as a quarter of a million Cornish people had left for overseas in the century after 1815, with an almost equal number having departed for other parts of the British Isles – to the coal mines of South Wales and the North of England, to the copper mines of Ireland, to the iron and coal mines of Scotland. At a time when the population of England and Wales was still rising, Cornwall's was in decline, a trend not reversed until the late 1960s.

Alongside Ireland and southern Italy, Cornwall was one of the great emigration regions of Europe. Today, there are millions of people of Cornish descent the world over. Many of these are proud of their Cornish roots and still consider themselves to be Cousin Jacks and Jennies.

There are numerous Cornish Associations in North America, Australia, New Zealand, South Africa, and even one in Cuba. They organise all kinds of events, including conferences and 'gatherings' where people travel for hundreds of miles to meet others of Cornish descent and to visit sites – such as Grass Valley in California – with Cornish connections. In 'Australia's Little Cornwall' there is even a biennial Kernewek Lowender, advertised as 'the World's largest Cornish Festival'.

Kernewek Lowender in South Australia's Yorke Peninsula celebrates cultural connections with Cornwall – you can even buy a pasty there!

Cornish-Australians participate in a grand 'Celtic Parade' at Glen Innes in New South Wales, Australia.

feasts & festivals,
sports & pastimes

and for exercise of the body,

and for exercise of the minde...

'Pastimes to delight the minde...

RICHARD CAREW
SURVEY OF CORNWALL
1602

In Cornwall, feasts and festivals, and sports and pastimes, have always been an element of community life, combining leisure pursuits with religious observance and folkloric ritual. Even today, despite the ever-present influences of television, the internet and other distractions, such activities remain an important part of Cornish culture.

As Anne Treneer observed in her *Schoolhouse in the Wind* (first published in 1944), in which she described life in Gorran and Caerhays, Cornish customs were linked to the rhythms of the year and the pattern of the seasons:

'Our feasts and diversions depended on the weather and the church, the two being intertwined: Winter with Christmas, Spring with Easter; Summer with Whitsuntide and Trinity; Autumn with St Michael and All Angels and the Harvest Festival'.

More than fifty years on this is still true, with a multiplicity of activities old and new fixed firmly in the Cornish calendar. Here, then, is a sketch of the Cornish Year.

Until very recently it was commonplace for 'guise dancers' or 'mummers' to welcome the New Year by going round their villages in disguise, acting out scenes from plays or songs. In one or two places the custom survives, and the tradition of disguise (including the blackening of faces) continues in events such as the Padstow Darkie Days and the St Ives Guise Dancing on Feast Monday.

Illustration by Sarah Dearlove, BA (Hons) Illustration, Falmouth College of Arts

'Feasts' are very Cornish events, celebrations linked to the Saint's Days of parishes and towns, such as those of St Day, St Just-in-Penwith, Redruth, Crowan or Lanlivery. In February, the St Ives and St Columb Major Feast events include hurling, a sport once enjoyed across Cornwall. Historically, there were two kinds of hurling, to goal or to country, the game consisting of chasing and throwing a small silver ball, often engraved with a Cornish motto:

'Gware wheag yu gware teg'

Hurling at St Columb takes place on Shrove Tuesday. The two sides, the 'Townmen' and the 'Countrymen' each have their own goals – two miles apart. The silver ball is engraved with the motto – *'Town and Country do your best – For in this parish I must rest'.*

In 1602 Richard Carew wrote: '*In these matches the hurlers take their next way over hilles, dales, hedges, ditches; yea, and thorow bushes, briers, mires, plashes and rivers whatsoever; so you shall sometimes see twenty or thirty lie tugging together in water, scrambling and scratching for the ball*'. Today hurling is not quite so violent but on Shrove Tuesday at St Columb the shop fronts are still boarded up to prevent damage.

Rugby football has inherited many of the features of hurling and today is recognised as a very 'Cornish' sport. Different areas are fiercely loyal to their local teams – such as Launceston ('the Cornish All Blacks'), Penzance and Newlyn ('the Pirates'), and Redruth ('the Reds') – but all Cornwall comes together to support the Cornish team in the County Championships. By early spring, the Cornish team will have played its qualifying games and its supporters ('Trelawny's Army') will know whether they are once again on the road to Twickenham. In 1991 some 40,000 people, almost ten percent of Cornwall's population, made their way to see the Cornish team defeat Yorkshire in the Final. A new saying became famous: 'Last one to leave Cornwall, turn out the light!'

Paul Watts

'Fair play is good play'

Ann Trevenen Jenkin

People of all ages – but with youngsters prominent – walk across the dunes at Perranporth on St Piran's Day, the 5th March. The black and white flag of St Piran is today seen all across Cornwall, but it is especially in evidence on St Piran's Day.

St Piran's Day, 5th March, also enjoys widespread support across Cornwall, and is today perhaps our most significant Cornish festival. St Piran's flag, the symbol of Cornwall, flies throughout the year but 5th March is reserved for special commemoration of this important Saint. There is an annual pilgrimage (which includes many schoolchildren) across the sand dunes at Perranporth, and there is also a parade through the streets of Truro. Elsewhere in Cornwall hundreds of people – including many youngsters – participate in upwards of thirty special events. Further afield, in North America, Australia, and New Zealand, there are also gatherings to celebrate the Feast of St Piran.

Another important happening in March is the Cornish Music Festival, held in Truro with over 2,000 participants from Cornwall and beyond. Its motto is Bedhens Kernow en Kessenyans/Let Cornwall be in Harmony. The year 2000 marked the ninetieth anniversary of the Festival's foundation. Its success mirrors the popularity of music-making throughout Cornwall. Other events, such as the brass and silver band festival at Bugle and the music festivals at St Endellion and Camborne, all involve young people and make a great contribution to community life. Younger composers, like Eselde Pierce from St Keverne or Russell Pascoe from Truro, are producing new work for the Millennium based on Cornish themes. Cornish youth brass and wind bands, such as those of Bodmin and St Keverne, or Carrick and Triggshire, have outstanding records both here and across the Tamar.

Ann Trevenen Jenkin

Spring brings warmer days, with an abundance of flowers in the Cornish countryside and in Cornish gardens (such as Heligan and Trebah, Trewithen and Caerhays) which are open to the public. On Good Friday, 'trigging' (from the Cornish word 'trig', an 'ebbing of the sea') takes place on the Helford River, when it is the custom to collect small shellfish such as limpets and winkles. Easter itself is an important religious festival, in Cornwall as elsewhere, with many churches and chapels displaying their 'Easter Gardens' – Christ's tomb, surrounded by primroses and moss.

On the last Saturday in April, Camborne celebrates its Trevithick Day, a festival dedicated to the commemoration of the famous inventor of the steam locomotive, Richard Trevithick, and Cornwall's great industrial heritage. Although quite new, Trevithick Day is already an important part of the Cornish calendar, admired especially for its grand parade of traction engines through the town. Not to be outdone, Redruth (Camborne's great rival) has its Murdoch Day, held on the weekend of the old Redruth Whitsun Fair, which celebrates William Murdoch, the first man to use gas to for house-lighting. Murdoch House, where the experiment was first tried, can still be found in Redruth, now a centre for education and community activities.

The Lost Gardens of Heligan, near Mevagissey, have been restored in recent years. This is a wonderful example of a Cornish garden, full of exotic plants from Asia, Australia, New Zealand and elsewhere which it would be very difficult to grow in most other areas of Britain. Parts of Heligan and other Cornish gardens have an almost 'tropical" jungle-like atmosphere.

David Hastilow

Steve Tanner

The grand parade of traction engines at Camborne's Trevithick Day is a stirring reminder of Cornwall's premier place in the history of steam engineering. People from all over Cornwall and beyond flock to join Camborne's celebration of Richard Trevithick.

Paul Watts

With the arrival of May, some of the most famous Cornish festivals occur. The first is May Day at Padstow, when everywhere is decorated with bluebells and cowslips. The insistent beat of the drum and the haunting melody, once heard, are never forgotten, nor is the strange twirling 'Oss taunted by the teaser. The festival's origins are lost in the mists of time but the dying and re-birth of the 'Oss signify the death of winter and the coming of summer. Despite the thousands of visitors, it is a special Padstow celebration.

May Day at Padstow, with the 'Obby 'Oss making its traditional 'tour' of the town, accompanied by the teaser, musicians playing accordians and drums, and hundreds of spectators, many of them singing the Padstow May Day Song:

Paul Watts

'Unite and Unite, and let us all unite
For Summer is acome unto day,
And whither we are going we will all unite
In the merry morning of May'

There are two rival 'Osses', the Blue Ribbon or 'Peace' 'Oss that makes its first appearance from the Institute at 10am on May Day, followed by the Old 'Red' 'Oss which emerges from the Golden Lion public house at 11am.

A week later, on 8th May, it is Helston's turn to greet the arrival of summer, with its Furry or Flora Day. The oldest part of the ceremony is the Hal an Tow, with its strange characters in colourful costumes, the slaying of the Dragon by St Michael, and the Town Crier's welcome in both Cornish and English. From early morning to late afternoon, a succession of dancers take to the streets. About 1500 children, all dressed in white and wearing lilies of the valley, participate in the Children's Dance. Even more spectacular is the 12 o'Clock Dance, where many dancers have new outfits and the women huge colourful hats.

Helston's Flora or Furry Day. The first dance through the town is at 7am, followed by the Hal-an-Tow ceremony, and then the Children's Dance at 10.30am. At 12 o'clock sharp, the clock strikes at the Guildhall and immediately the band begins to play the famous tune known the world over. The dancers really do go 'in and out of the houses' in what writer Douglas Williams has called *'an exciting blend of theatre and history'*, as they travel their traditional routes through the town. Later in the day, there is also a 5pm dance.

Paul Watts

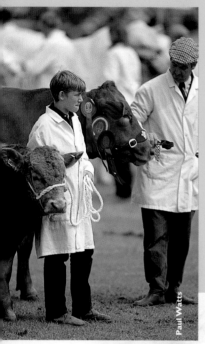

The arrival of summer is a cue for all kinds of feasts and festivals, sports and pastimes. Miners' Gala Days are held in Camborne-Redruth and at Geevor (near St Just) to remind us of Cornwall's mining heritage here and the world over. The Royal Cornwall Show, which can be traced back to the Cornwall Agricultural Association founded in 1793, is held at Wadebridge in early June and celebrates the important role of farming in Cornish life. But its appeal is to all sections of the community. Now one of the biggest shows in Britain, it routinely attracts over 100,000 visitors. There are marquees for plants and animals, stalls selling everything from cars and farm machinery to double-glazing and footwear, together with demonstrations, displays, competitions and judging in the main rings.

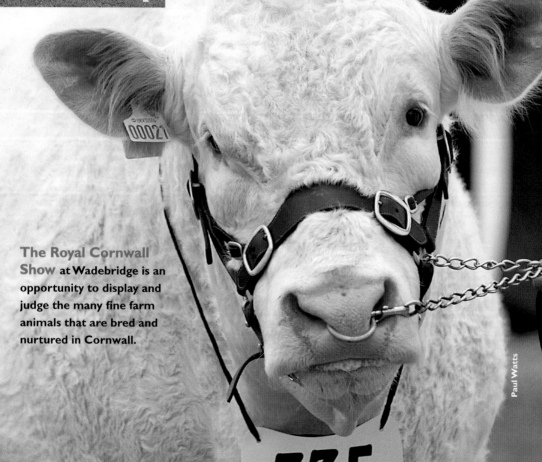

The Royal Cornwall Show at Wadebridge is an opportunity to display and judge the many fine farm animals that are bred and nurtured in Cornwall.

Golowan, the Feast of St John, is celebrated at Penzance, a recent revival of the old Corpus Christi Fair held on the Thursday, Friday and Saturday of the week following Trinity Sunday. The Saturday, Mazey Day, is the highlight of the festival, when a huge parade is staged through the streets of Penzance. St John's Eve, 23rd June, is the Christianised version of an ancient pagan festival when bonfires were lit to venerate the power of the sun and to mark the victory of summer over winter. Midsummer bonfires, as they are known, were still popular in the mid-nineteenth century but had almost died out by the early twentieth century, when they were revived by the Old Cornwall Societies. Today, there are huge bonfires on St John's Eve at places such as Carn Brea, near Redruth, and Kit Hill, near Callington, when into the flames are cast both good and useless weeds, with a prayer in Cornish for safe crops and a good harvest.

June is also the month when the Cornish rebels of 1497 are remembered in ceremonies on the 27th at St Keverne and at Bodmin, together with Hyde Park in London – the site of Tyburn gallows where the rebel leaders, Michael Joseph An Gof and Thomas Flamank, were executed after the battle of Blackheath. A week or so later, on or about 7th July, Bodmin Riding takes place in the town of that name. Associated traditionally with the return of St Petroc's bones from Brittany to Cornwall, Bodmin Riding today is linked closely with remembrance of the Cornish Prayer Book Rebellion of 1549. Amongst the events is the mock hanging of the mayor, echoing the execution of the rebel Mayor of Bodmin, Nicholas Boyer, in 1549.

Although only recently revived, Golowan is already an indispensable part of the Cornish scene. On Mazey Day, Penzance is alive with colour, movement and the sound of music making.

Photos: Mike Newman

John Knill was present at the first Knill Ceremony, near St Ives in 1801, and left money for gifts for those taking part as well as to pay for a sumptuous dinner. Critics claimed, however, that he was an ally of the local smugglers and that he had created the monument as a convenient daymark to aid their smuggling activities.

Still in July, is the Knill Ceremony, held every five years on or near 25 July (St James's Day) at the monument built at St Ives in 1782 by John Knill, a native of Callington but Mayor of St Ives in 1767. First instituted in 1801, the ceremony consists of ten little girls, two elderly widows and a fiddler who dance around the monument to the tune of the Cornish Furry Dance. The Furry Dance is also often performed at the many Carnivals held up and down Cornwall during the summer months, and at these and other events are sometimes displays of Cornish wrestling. Wearing their distinctive unbleached linen or canvas jackets, and watched over by adjudicators called 'sticklers', today's Cornish wrestlers are the inheritors of an ancient Celtic sport that survives now in Cornwall and Brittany.

The summer months are also a time for water sports. Pilot Gig Racing, a survival from the days when gigs would race out to ships off-shore in the hope of being the first to deliver a pilot on board, is hugely popular in Cornwall. Almost every Cornish cove, together with the Isles of Scilly, has its own gig (some with all-women crews), such as the 'Anne Glanville' of Saltash, the 'Rival' of Fowey, and the 'Energetic' of Porthleven. Surfing and surf life-saving have also become major water activities in Cornwall, with locations such as Newquay and Bude attracting international attention as venues for prestigious competitions, the Cornish answers to places like Hawaii and Australia's Bondi Beach.

Although nineteenth-century Cornish Methodists often disapproved of Cornish Wrestling, it survived in Cornwall and was taken overseas as a popular Cornish sport. Today, wrestling is seen as an important element of Cornwall's Celtic identity.

Paul Watts

Paul Watts

The surf of North Cornwall has caught international interest and established the region as a venue for surfing and life-saving competitions.

The power and excitement of a Cornish gig-racing competition is conveyed in this action photograph.

Frank Gibson

The 'Crying the neck'
ceremony survived into
the twentieth-century to
be preserved and re-
enacted annually by the
Federation of Old
Cornwall Societies.
In 1951 the ceremony
was observed at
Gwarthandrea, Mawgan-
in-Meneage, where the
following ritual was
recorded:

First Harvester:
'I have'n,
I have'n,
I have'n'
Second Harvester:
'What have 'ee?
What have 'ee?
What have 'ee?'
First Harvester:
'The Neck!
The Neck!
The Neck!'
All: 'Hooray!'

Summer is also set aside for other sports, such as cricket. Many Cornish villages have their own cricket teams, and Troon has regularly performed well in the country-wide village team competition, as has the Cornwall side in the 'minor counties' championship. Golf is another favourite sport. St Mellion is one of several Cornish courses of international standard, and St Enodoc was made famous by its association with the poet, Sir John Betjeman. Golf is also popular with young people in Cornwall. In 1999, for example, Scott Godfrey, then 18 years old and a member of the St Enodoc club, was selected to play for Great Britain and Ireland in what turned out to be their successful encounter with the Continent of Europe team.

The arrival of autumn is a signal for harvest festivals. 'Crying the Neck', an ancient Celtic fertility rite which marked the end of the harvest, lingered into the twentieth century to be revitalised in Christianised form by the Old Cornwall Societies. More obviously Christian is the Harvest Festival service itself, today familiar all over the world but first formalised in the nineteenth century by the famous Rev Robert Stephen Hawker of Morwenstow.

The Harvest Festival
service was created
by the Rev Robert
Stephen Hawker
of Morwenstow.

Ann Trevenen Jenkin

The first Saturday in September sees the ceremony of the bards of the Gorseth Kernow (Cornish Gorsedd), held each year in a different part of Cornwall. Revived from an old custom in 1928, and linked to similar ceremonies in Wales and Brittany, the Gorseth consists today of about 500 living bards. They have each been invited to join the Gorseth on account of some outstanding contribution to the life of Cornwall, and have agreed to uphold the national Celtic spirit of Cornwall. The Gorseth ceremony is extremely popular, with visitors from all over the world. School students take part as attendants or dancers, and many teachers encourage their students to enter the various Gorseth competitions. Hot on the heels of the Gorseth, during the second week of October, is the *Lowender Peran* at Perranporth. First held in 1979, it draws musicians, dancers and other participants from across the Celtic world, from Brittany, Wales, Scotland, Ireland, and the Isle of Man.

Now often regarded as the most important Cornish cultural organisation, Gorseth Kernow commands international respect and has within its ranks bards who have done much to enhance and promote Cornwall's unique way of life.

A stunning example of the Christmas lights at Newlyn.

And so to Christmas, the last great festival of the year, marked in Cornwall with distinctive activities such as Tom Bawcock's Eve at Mousehole, the Cornish Carols of Thomas Merritt, and the Service of Nine Lessons and Carols (first instituted in Truro Cathedral), reminding us of the important Cornish contribution to European and indeed global religion and culture.

Choristers at Truro Cathedral, in front of the Christmas Tree.

The Great Hall decked out for **Christmas at Cotehele**, the National Trust's property near Calstock, above the River Tamar.

Cornwall looks forward

In this chapter,
the young people
of Cornwall think
about the present
and take a look
into the future.
Drawn from a huge volume of contributions
from school children across Cornwall, from
Morwenstow in the far north and Millbrook in the
south east to Mullion on the Lizard peninsula
and St Just in the far west, this representative
selection includes
work from those
as young as five
to seventeen year
-olds soon to go
to university.

The youngest children at Key Stage I in the National Curriculum *(up to seven years of age)* were asked to write about or illustrate the theme 'Work and Play' while junior pupils at Key Stage 2 *(seven to eleven years)* were given 'Our Village/Town', Secondary school students at Key Stage 3 *(aged 11 to 14 years)* have written on the theme 'Our Community in Cornwall', while those aged 14 to 18 years tackled 'The Future Economy of Cornwall'.

In each of the categories, what is remarkable is the desire to take full advantage of the opportunities and new technologies of the future while at the same time preserving and enhancing all that is best about Cornwall. Timothy Day, aged six, wants to be a farmer and says that 'I'll work by the sea'. But his cows will be milked by a 'robot milker' and his cooker will be regulated by a computer. Alice Weghofer, also aged six, will be an intergalactic 'flying dentist'. William Bryant, another six year old, wants to be a funeral director but even his profession will be assisted by the latest in computer technology.

Contributors at Key Stage 2 emphasise the warmth of community life. Sonia Drew tells us that Praze-an-Beeble is a friendly place with its village fair, nice school and local shops. Samantha Hamilton, from Barncoose in the heart of the Camborne-Redruth former mining district, enthuses over 'Deserted mine stacks standing proud' and the 'mysteries of Cornish myths and legends', welcoming the tourists who come to find out more about Cornwall. Rosie Monies, from Zennor, is concerned for the future of her village. There are improvements she would like to see but she wants to protect the small scale environment that gives Zennor its special qualities.

At Wadebridge, Amy Meldrum hopes for 'new parks and playgrounds and a cinema in 3D' and thinks that new technology will make teachers redundant. Fumeless hover cars will put an end to pollution. Ladock in 2050, says Craig Milling, will be a quiet village without cars and litter, a haven where people will still consume 'traditional Cornish food and drink in the local pub' but will communicate with the outside world by email rather than letter. At Millbrook, Jasmine Griffiths and Jennie Bond identify the shortcomings of today but ask 'why can't it be a dazzling Millbrook tomorrow?'.

Key Stage 3 contributors stress similar themes, Chris Wilson, from Truro, sees Cornwall becoming a politically independent part of the European Union and the Commonwealth, with its traditional industries revitalised by Objective 1 funding and Cornish expertise sought the world over. Miriam Jenkin, from Mullion, pictures a Cornish 'Community Dome' where people can attend classes in everything from the Cornish language to Philosophy, 'Learn more to enrich your future' is Cornwall's new catch cry. The Dome provides thousands of jobs, and one of its many roles is the rehabilitation of criminals. Ceri Tindale, from Roseland, is insistent that 'the spirit of Cornwall shall never die!!'. Talei Lakeland, from St Austell, also envisages an independent Cornwall where the celebration of tradition and identity exists side-by-side with adoption of the latest technology and preservation of the environment. For Faith Coles, from Launceston, 'Cornwall is a separate place... not just another county, it's special'. For Merryn Pearce, from the Roseland, 'Some day Cornwall shall reign again in her former glory/Some day Cornwall shall lift her head high/In industry, spirit and beauty'.

In writing about the future economy of Cornwall, the older students also wish to match economic progress with the promotion of the Cornish identity. Fiona Price, from Bodmin, sees the establishment of a Cornish university as the key to both social and economic development in Cornwall. She says, 'We want to educate our youngsters at our own university'. Laura Hancock, also from Bodmin, is proud of 'our Celtic nation' and argues that the establishment of a university would keep 'the Cornish spirit alive', a view echoed by Amanda Henry (again from Bodmin) who wants to 'preserve our rich cultural background and natural Celtic beauty whilst bringing Cornwall forward for the next millennium'.

Tegan Smale, aged 7, St Tudy School.

work & play

When I grow up I will be a farmer. I'll work by the sea. My tractor will be enormous like no other tractor you will see today. I will milk cows with a robot milker. I will rear the chickens for their meat outside because it is nicer for them outside. I will catch them and cook them in my computer cooker.

In my spare time I will be typing on the computer and playing games. I will go for lots of walks with my children. We will go in the woods and we will see people planting lots of trees. Some of the old trees they will cut down and put new ones instead. I'll go to the beach and run around with my children. There will be lots of waves.

Timothy Day, aged 7, St Mark's School, Morwenstow.

I would grow big big figs to feed my family. Figs in 2000 will be as big as melons

Ollie marshall
5 years

Ollie Marshall,
aged 5,
Mousehole School.

In the new Millenium

In the future I might see

A car with wings

or a robot with stretchy arms.

A dome house

or a garden with grass ten feet tall

or a forest covered by a dome

A garden on the moon

or a garden on top of a roof

or some shoes with mega boosters

or a bike with an exhoust pipe at the front

A computer as big as ants.

Kyle Knipe, aged 6, Mousehole School.

A day in the life of Alice Weghofer aged 26.

I put on my space powered backpack, to go to the moon. My job used to be a pilot. I had a mask, and people said that I looked really scary! I didn't like that much, so I changed my job. Now I'm a flying dentist. I go around the universe cleaning aliens teeth. Well, some don't have any! The one I liked best was called 811. It looked like a bit like a doughnut turned sideways, except it had horns and arms and legs. This is the best job in the world, although I did really want to scar people.
by Alice Weghofer aged 6

Alice Weghofer,
aged 7,
Stratton Primary School.

Work in the Future

In the future a teacher has a robot who helps the teacher to help the children. The children have a computer each and some children work at school and some at home because they could take the computers home.

**Danny Runnalls,
aged 7,
St Mabyn School.**

In the future I think when I grow up I'm going to be a funeral director. I will have a computer in the car and when I put the computer card in the car I can tell the car to go forwards, backwards, left and right. I will bury people after they have died. People are much older when they die now because they eat healthy food and get lots of exercise. In my car there is a television which I can watch before the funerals.

William Bryant, aged 6, St Mark's School, Morwenstow.

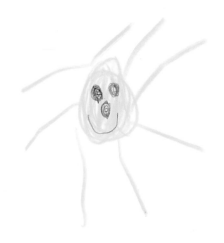

This Will be our new Millennium Park.
This Park is called mouse Park and it will
have a Slide and it will have a Water Slide
and it will have a swing.

Jordan Moore, aged 6, Bosvigo School, Truro.

our town, our village

My Village

I see the stone church sparkling.
The bright sea crashing.
Holiday children building.
I hear the holiday people biking.
Noisy children chatting.
Church bells ringing.
Poundstock is my village.

**Duncan Cox, aged 7,
Bude Junior School.**

My Town Bude

My town Bude is really great,
A seaside town you could not hate,
The sky is nearly always blue,
It honestly will astound you.

Bude is a peaceful place,
Moving along at a steady pace.
It hardly ever speeds ahead,
Just carries on, or so it's said.

The waves crashing on the shore,
You can hear them growl and roar.
The sandy beach, with a few stones.
and lots of people eating ice cream cones.

Over the cliffs a beautiful view,
Lots to see for me and you,
When there's a bright shining sun,
We shall have lots of fun.

Bude it has something for all,
Leisure centre, beach and a swimming pool,
There's the canal, museum and a library,
How much more is there to see!

There's the town with lots of shops,
And High Street I think it's tops,
There's the 18 hole golf course,
Or you can go riding on a horse.

Now I think we're nearly done,
Can we get it in, in one.
The red sun setting over the sea,
Isn't Bude a nice place to be.

Desra Slinn, aged 11, Bude Junior School.

Our Village

I live in Praze an Beeble. In my village there is a Post office and a pub and a pasty Shop. Sometimes in the village you can ride on your bikes. It is a nice place. In the village we have a fair. There are a lot of people in the village. My school in the village is nice and all the Teachers are nice. I have some friend in the village.

by Sonia Drew

Sonia Drew, aged 8, Crowan CP School.

Remains of Cam brea castle sits high on the hill for all to see.

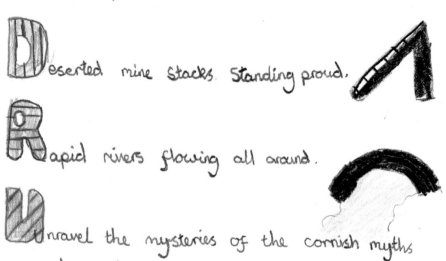

Early rising sun rolling across the wonderful landscapes.

Deserted mine stacks standing proud.

Rapid rivers flowing all around.

Unravel the mysteries of the cornish myths and legends.

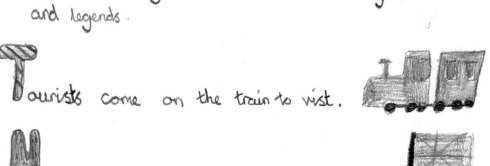

Tourists come on the train to visit.

Historical buildings can be seen everywhere.

Samantha Hamilton, aged 10, Barncoose School.

My Village

I see the beach with gold sand and waves crashing.
Overjoyed children playing.
On the beach pebbles crinkling.
I hear overhead seagulls are screeching.
Tanned lifeguards are whistling.
Shaking dogs barking.
I love the darling countryside moving.
The little birds loving.
The beautiful views winking.
Crackington Haven is my village.

Isabel Nash, aged 8, Bude Junior School.

St Gennys

St Gennys is a very old village but modern and a busy place.

There are three Iron Age forts. They are really old. In the parish there is a silver band, a ladies choir, a surf club and a snooker club.

For the millennium the village is making a magazine called 'A Hundred Years of Photos in St Gennys'. The ladies of the parish are making a needlework tapestry all about St Gennys. For the future we have a beautiful place with a lot of wildlife, cliffs, and a beach. Although we want our village to stay a busy happy place, we must conserve it.

St Gennys is a beautiful place and we don't want to spoil a really special place, we must conserve it. The beach is the prettiest feature in St Gennys. The cliffs are very nice when it is sunset and we don't want to spoil it. The village has a post office - shop - church - 2 chapels - river - beach - woodland - small tennis court - parish hall - school - school house - coastal path, beach shops - pub. We want St Gennys as it is. What we have is very special we must KEEP IT SO!

Jodie Savill, aged 11, Jacobstow Primary School.

Zennor

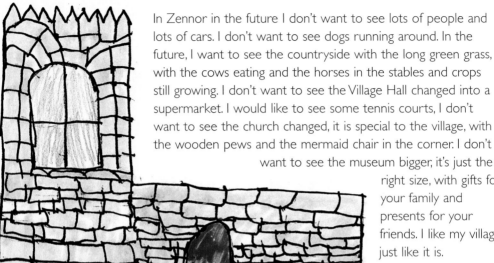

In Zennor in the future I don't want to see lots of people and lots of cars. I don't want to see dogs running around. In the future, I want to see the countryside with the long green grass, with the cows eating and the horses in the stables and crops still growing. I don't want to see the Village Hall changed into a supermarket. I would like to see some tennis courts, I don't want to see the church changed, it is special to the village, with the wooden pews and the mermaid chair in the corner. I don't want to see the museum bigger, it's just the right size, with gifts for your family and presents for your friends. I like my village just like it is.

**Rosie Monies,
aged 10,
Nancledra School**

Golitha Falls

Golitha Falls are just outside Liskeard. The bubbling River Fowey flows through the beech wood there.

Watch the falls flow beautifully as they journey to the sea.
Hear them roar, hear them crash, watch out for the splash.
Cascading crystal clear waters, tumbling over mossy boulders.
Listen to the pebbles rumble, now a swish, now a mumble.
Sing their noisy bubbly song, babbling loudly all day long.
See the darting black fish sway, swimming fast, swimming away.
On the water floats a leaf, sneaking silently away like a thief.
Overhead the branches creak while wary squirrel takes a peek.

Bring a picnic, bring a drink, sit still and listen at the water's brink

Donna Leng, aged 10, Liskeard Junior School.

Wadebridge in the future

Wadebridge in the future
Is the place I'd like to be.
New parks and playgrounds
and a cinema in 3D.

The play equipment is futuristic,
the slides as high as can be,
the roundabout goes faster and faster
until its time for my tea.

The schools are no longer needed
The teachers are out of a job
Every things done by Computer,
And we don't even need Mrs Lobb.

The hover car has been invented,
there's no more polution or fumes,
No more complaints about speed bumps,
for now the car just zooms.

by Amy Meldrum

Amy Meldrum, aged 10, Wadebridge CP School.

St. Stephens.

Very good is our village,
I am always in there.
It is quiet, peaceful, relaxing and lovely.
Lovely Church with flowers around it.
Living there would be a treat.
Always going to the park.
Glorious Shops with good toys,
Every day bits and bobs too.

By Treve
Murley

Treve Murley, aged 8, St Stephen Churchtown CP School.

Kilkhampton is excellent because it is a friendly village.
I like being in Kilkhampton, we have lots of friends.
Living in Kilkhampton is important to us because it is our home.
Kilkhampton has an old, beautiful and friendly school.
Happy People make it a special place.
An extraordinary village to live in.
Magical memories when we are older.
Personal village where we know each other.
Twinkling sky at night.
Orangey sun sinking into the sea.
Nowhere is better.

Briony Cann, aged 9;
Daniel Tolson, aged 8;
Ashley Thomas, aged 8;
Thomas Johnson, aged 7,
Kilkhampton Junior & Infants School.

My Millennium

The Millennium will be a very special time in our school. We are having a new hall and new classes. I am also going to the big school in a few more years.
I want to be a lead guitarist and learn to play really good. Just like Noel Gallagher for a pop band. I can't play but I will learn to play the guitar. I will go to the Millennium Dome when it opens.

Jack Ninnis, aged 9
St Just Primary School.

Veryan

I'm a little village in the South West of Cornwall,
My name is Veryan, my husband's Portloe,
My Children Pendower and Carne,
Live with us near a barn.

I hold the longest grave in Cornwall,
The legendary Round Houses,
And the W.I. Hall.

My village green has always been seen,
My old, old wood has a very bent tree,
Her name of course is Eileen.

I hold a sports club, a shop and park,
My school is cool,
And my church is dark.

Veryan Green is like a brother to me,
He holds an art gallery,
And we make a really good team.

Wei Adams, aged 9, Veryan CE VA School.

Protect Pipe Well!

The new-look Liskeard looks lovely but what about the ancient Pipe Well? It has become a place for people to sit and drop litter and only a few years ago it was a place where I stopped to play.

I remember one very hot summer's day when I was there with my little sister. Unable to keep cool, we stood looking at the four pipes dripping, dropping, cold clear crystal water in the dark damp well below. The creamy coloured stone surrounding the well felt like marble, soft, smooth to touch. We took off our sandals. We grabbed the black gate in front of the well and dipped our feet into the cool refreshing water flowing from the pipes.

We squealed and giggled as drip, drop, the cooling waters touched our hot dusty feet. We caught the cold water in our cupped hands, forming little puddles and splashing them at each other's face, like foamy surf from the sea.

Nobody would stop there now to admire the well, even the water looks dirty. We used to pretend it was a tomb with someone buried there, a haunted place, just to scare others away. It does its own scaring now!

Jessica O'Carroll, aged 10, Liskeard Junior School.

Ladock 2050

My ancestors have lived in Ladock for over two hundred years. I am now a man over 60 years old. I have been away from Ladock for 40 years. As I walk down the road, it is strangely quiet. For no cars drive along. I have left my transport in a special park. The granite church is still here, standing proud on top of the hill. Next door is the village school, also quiet and strange, it is now a museum and I am pleased to see some of my work on display.

For lunch I visit The Falmouth Arms, to sample some traditional Cornish food and drink. I sit back and remember my Nan's pasties. There is no Post Office or shop. Every one nowadays uses emails and computers. The Red Kiosk, the old telephone box, is just a focal point, with flowers around it.

The village itself hasn't changed. No new houses, the river is still running through the middle, crystal clear water. There is no mess or litter anywhere, a real joy to see. Soon it is time for me to go, I walk to my aerocar, and begin my journey home to my family on the moon.

Craig Milling, aged 11, Ladock CP School.

Millbrook's Millennium

Jennie Bond, aged 9, Millbrook School.

If now it is a scruffy skate park,
Why can't it be a spectacular skate park tomorrow?

If now it is a dreadful dam,
Why can't it be a delightful dam tomorrow?

If now it is a boring boatyard,
Why can't it be a brilliant boatyard tomorrow?

If now it is a lousy lake,
Why can't it be a luxury lake tomorrow?

If now it is a worthless wildlife,
Why can't it be a wonderful wildlife tommorow?

If now it is a filthy football pitch,
Why can't it be a fantastic football pitch tommorow?

If now it is a messy mill.
Why can't it be a superb mill tomorrow?

If now it is all of these things,
Why can't it be like this tomorrow?

Jasmine Griffiths, aged 9, Millbrook School.

Millbrook 2000

our community in Cornwall

A Voice

Cornwall
   living in the heart of Cornwall is happiness
Millennium
   it's not all about technology
Environment
   it's beautiful, but it's going..... going......
Money
   use it for life's essentials
Cornwall
   it's my home, but it's changing

Jenny McFarland, aged 12, Mullion School.

Isles of Scilly

My favourite place in Cornwall is the Isles of Scilly. It might not be attached to Britain, but it is still Cornwall.

Tresco has such wonderful scenery and beautiful plants. There are lots of different types of birds on Tresco and if you are quiet they will come really close to you. Also on the Isles of Scilly there is lots of wildlife like seals, puffins, jellyfish, dolphins, whales and lots more.

On the Scilly Isles there is only one big town placed on St Mary's and it is no bigger than Launceston but there are a lot of choices in shops etc. Gift shops, ice cream shops, antique shops, sport shops and other shops like that.

There are also public showers which are really expensive, there is a museum which tells the history of the islands and the beaches are beautiful, no litter, the sand is smooth and the ocean is really clear.

The reason I like the Isles of Scilly is because it is so peaceful and there is no pollution.

Fiona Ellacott, aged 13, Launceston College.

Through a Millennium Keyhole

In the future I can see,
The Millennium village of St Hilary.
The stained glass church,
The golden cockerel on it's perch,
Gravestones which used to stand
So tall and proud,
All knocked down and lying on the ground.

A floor like a checker board,
A chair waiting for the coming Lord,
Are where the gravestones used to be,
In the grand village of St Hilary.
The cockerel from the church,
Is the crown of the bird on its alien perch.

The people who were here,
Were friendly and tidy.
But now there are litter bugs,
With long antennas,
Eyes full of hexagons and hate.
They lay traps with bait.

The old windy lanes,
Are now staright and flat.
Instead of bumpy old cormac,
The roads are hard and plastic.
The oaks and elms are gone for good,
Plastic is taking over, there is no wood!

Ruth Walden, aged 10, St Hilary School.

Future Map of Cornwall

I took a map of Cornwall
And I showed it to my friends
'Imagine Cornwall in years to come
All the changes our future sends'

My first friend took the paper
'We'll all drive solar powered cars
We'll be connected to the internet
And have holidays on Mars'

I showed it to my second friend
'We won't have to go to school
We'll all have virtual teachers
And there won't be any rules'

I gave the paper to another friend
'You want to know what the future holds?
We can't – it's us that make it happen
We have to watch as it unfolds

This isn't the future we're talking of
This is about our dreams and hopes
Wherever we are in the future
Right now we're still learning the ropes'

I looked at my map of Cornwall
What my friend had said was true
I saw my home, covered in questions
But our dreams were shining through

**Tara O' Sullivan, aged 13,
Mullion School.**

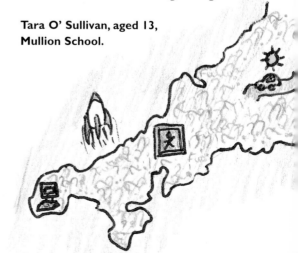

Why Cornwall is Special to Me

Cornwall is a separate place, cut off from England by the Tamar, the rest surrounded by sea. We have our own music, our own festivals and events, and our own culture.

We even have our own language, saved from disappearing by a small handful of people in Cornwall, and learnt by a scattering of others in foreign countries.

There are now many large built up areas here, but the typical small Cornish villages still huddle in green, wooded valleys or straggle down steep, wild hillsides. Grey slate roofed cottages nestle on a headland while powerful waves smack themselves against the rocky cliffs. Trawlers chug out of the busy little harbours and fishermen set their nets ready for a big shoal of mackerel or pilchards, herring or skate. Others throw out the big, stiff rope pots for catching lobsters or crabs. Sometimes they can not go out fishing as the calm blue green sea turns grey and is laced with white foam, as the blue, cloudless sky turns black as thunder and rain pelts down in a thick soaking sheet accompanied by flashing lightning. The waves grow to ten times the size and crash on the harbour walls, trying in vain to get past the barrier. These storms are truly magical if you get the chance to watch one from the safety of the small cottages. They are wild and savage, and you suddenly feel very small.

There are lots of wild places. The moor is home to sheep and strong, sturdy ponies. Walking through tall bracken and gorse bushes you might see an adder or scare a grouse from their nest on the ground. Animals crop the grass until it makes a green carpet, springy under your feet. Standing on the High Tor, piled up with huge granite boulders thousands of centuries old, you might see or hear a skylark high overhead, darting through the air. Ancient remains of small villages remain, hut circles and tiny fields, stone circles and burial mounds for great chiefs long dead.

Cornwall is its own country. It has everything if you know where to look; wildness, sea, sandy beaches, high cliffs, narrow winding lanes, history. That's why it's so special to me, and it's what I love and know. Cornwall's not just another county, it's special.

Faith Coles, aged 13,

Launceston College.

Cornwall's future?

From the clank of a cornish beam engine,
To the click of a keyboard button.

From the sound of cornish voices singing,
To worldwide Techno pop.

From Colourful fishing boats launched from Cornish coves,
To the roar of factory ships hauling "Silver darlings"
from the sea.

From the shout of the farmer "Crying the neck"
To the clanging of machinery spraying chemicals over
the land

Kernow
BYS
Vyken

From the sound of cornish voices
To all accents under the sun

Ça
va?

From Tre, Pol and Pen
To Smith, Brown and Green

From "One and all"
To Who Knows What?

By Rosanna Richards

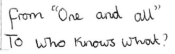

Rosanna Richards, aged 11, Mullion School.

The Cornish Revolution – a newspaper article from the future.

Proper Cornish people in Kernow are celebrating in the streets at the dawn of the Third Millennium! Cornwall is thriving!

We have taken this opportunity to reflect on Cornwall's recognisable triumph over the past few months, in which our county has made major advances.

In the late Second Millennium, us Cornish people became intolerant with the English government, especially its reluctance to fund our schools, businesses and industries. So we united to become an independent republic and dug a canal from the source of the River Tamar to the north coast; along the Cornwall/Devon border. We also demolished the Tamar Bridge while on strike. Kernow is now the island it deserves to be and our freedom is a physical reality!

Our second language will be Cornish and is taught in all schools. Editions of books – including this newspaper – are available in Cornish. The Cornish Pasty Trade is booming throughout the world– making our traditional fodder an internationally known delicacy and bringing in money!

Fishermen and women from Kernow are acknowledged as global heroes and heroines! They intend to save the world's staple fish species from extinction and set up several fish farms. their help is needed due to the mass overfishing by foreigners recently.

Also, Cornwall's many tin mines have been re-opened and made safe to supply the world with fine tin! Members of our community are helping to replant vast areas of forest and woodland. This has brought nature (very important to us) closer to our Cornish home. Our farms can expand freely in this environment and quality animals are bred in comfortable surroundings.

We have just exterminated BSE from our beef and banned genetically modified food, after a plea for safe food from the representatives of our newly elected county democracy.

The new world of Kernow is a place of great community life. Ancient festivals are celebrated every week when the whole county rejoices. This just shows how proud of our Cornish roots we are! Because of its independent status, Cornwall needs to keep up with and use new technology. This is the only way to keep on top of things and be able to provide jobs for everyone. Now, every adult is ensured a secure occupation.

All in all. these have been a few extraordinarily progressive months for Kernow, and the highlighting of its uniqueness. Here's to another thousand Cornish years!

Talei Lakeland, aged 12,
Poltair School.

Cornwall means to me...

Pixies, Pasties, Stargazey Pie,
China Clay pyramids piled up high,

Surfers, smugglers, sad seagulls cry,
Saffron cakes for tourists to try,

Flambards, fudge, St Piran's flags fly,
Fury as fishermen's livelihoods die,

Tintagel, Truro, Tamar flowing by,
Tin mines silhouetted against the sky,

Celts, clotted cream, a rugby try,
The spirit of Cornwall will never die!!

Ceri Tindale, aged 14,
Roseland Community School.

Our Community

The New Year's Resolution,
Is a tradition from the past,
But seldom but a week or two,
Do many of them last.

The millennium is the chance for us,
To make a better life,
To remove the violence from our streets,
All the trouble and the strife,

The problem of pollution,
Is one that we must face,
We must find a better solution,
To get rid of our waste.

Rebecca Davey, aged 13,
Pool School, Redruth.

Lowender Perran

I live near the town of Perranporth, on the north coast of Cornwall. It is mainly a tourist town, which the locals avoid in mid-season, but during the autumn, after all the shops have closed for the winter, Perranporth is brought to life by music and festivities.

Once a year, for five days at the end of October, Celtic bands and dance groups from Ireland, Scotland, Wales and Brittany, gather together in Perranporth for Lowender Perran. There are many festivities on all week, including a huge procession through the main street on the fourth day, Saturday.

The procession is the highlight of the week, and is made up of the Celtic bands, singers and dance groups, with the 'Obby 'Oss at the front. It comes down from the Ponsmere Hotel, where the festival is based, through the main street, and down to the sea front, where everyone branches off and plays in parks and squares.

Another main event is the ceilidh on Saturday night, where everyone turns up, to dance, drink, and meet people they haven't seen for years.

This is not the only event. All through the week there are dance, music and singing workshops, children's entertainers, stalls, and performances from local schools and groups. Everywhere you go, there is something going on, and everyone just has a great time. It is a fantastic week and one of my favourites of the year.

Naomi Moore, aged 13,
Newquay Tretherras School.

Cornwall – What will it be like in 100 years? – a wish

In 2099 there will be mines coming back, the pick swung, the pumps will pump again and miners will have a job again. South Crofty, Geevor and East Pool or Killifreth will work again with tin running out and money flowing in. The number of mines will increase, all because of Europe and the Objective 1 funding.

Maybe Europe was a good idea after all!

Cornwall will have a Parliament and, in time, will become a country and be independent. Cornwall will be like Australia or New Zealand, (not full of sheep), we will be part of the British Empire and not part of Britain 'directly'. The song by Cornishman Roger Bryant will be an anthem to Cornwall, just like 'Trelawny'. The song is called 'Cornish Lads'.

For Cornish lads are fishermen and Cornish lads are miners too,
but when the fish and tin are gone what are the Cornish lads to do?

'Trelawny' will become the national anthem of Cornwall. I think that Cornwall will have a dramatic breakthrough in something. Maybe in fishing or farming, mining or maybe rugby. It will bring major economic improvements and a rise in the standards of living. Fish will come to the shores and waters of Cornwall. Newlyn, Penzance, Mousehole and Looe will be revived from the tourist trade and into a 'proper industry'. I think that in years to come Tre... Pol... and Pen... will become family names all over the world with expertise in fishing and mining. Cornish recipes, such as pasties, yeast cake and hevvy cake, will become dishes all over the world.

Chris Wilson, aged 13, Truro School.

Cornwall In The Millennium

I think that Cornwall will become independent, like Ireland only a lot more successful. Cornwall will become famous for having some of the best rugby players in the world. People will be queuing up to get some tips from the world's best. Cornwall could then be able to afford to build massive theme parks. Cornwall's players would get millions, and they could give over half of it to charity. Eventually Cornish pasties would catch on and be given to the rugby winners. Other people would visit Cornwall because it is surrounded by coastline, so Cornwall could make more money with watersports.

Richard Barker, aged 13, Truro School.

Some Day

Some day the cliffs of Cornwall shall ring again,
Her past will be her future,
Some day Cornwall shall reign again in her former glory,
Some day Cornwall shall lift her head high
In industry, sport and beauty,
Some day the mines that have stood silent for so long
Shall stand silent no longer;
Some day;
Some day;
But what can we do until that day but sit and wait;
For the dream of millions to come true;
But to wait
Wait;
Wait;

Merryn Pearce, aged 13, Roseland Community School.

You go through the spinning doors, to enter a whole new world. Here, all the people in your community try to get their favourite attractions in the COMMUNITY DOME! The dome is so big you travel on to almost a flat escalator to get across.

Now when I said attractions, I didn't mean physical rollercoasters or any theme park kind of thing. No, I meant classes, both physical and mental. A popular class is the teaching of the Cornish language. People are finally trying to trace back to their roots and relive some traditions, instead of being like everyone else.

Another well attended class is Philosophy. People now really are great thinkers. People now care about how we all got to be where we are. Now people want to know the answers of all their children's questions.

All the classes apply with Cornwall's new phrase 'Learn more to enrich your future.'

One of the dome's new schemes has been congratulated on its true Christian spirit. Instead of a jail the dome has an area for ex-criminals who have been carefully monitored for half their sentence and spend the rest of it in the dome learning a new skill that they can use eventually outside the dome.

Saying that the dome provides thousands of jobs and pays people in a unique way that means having friends in high places isn't going to give you the better job. You work hard and you will be rewarded. This creates a fantastic environment for Cornish communities to live in.

Miriam Jenkin, aged13, Mullion School.

Narrow Is The Path

As Jake surveyed the ravaged desert of the Lizard Peninsula from his lofty pedestal atop the barrow at Roskruge Beacon the sight brought visions of his past with such clarity that the tears sprang to his eyes. When the Government officially sanctioned genetically modified foodstuffs, he had swiftly thrown his lot in with the supporters of the decision.

They had hired him, an able farmer, to help produce some of the modified plants from seed. With thoughtless abandon he had laboured, giving no thought to the unnatural monstrosities that grew from the seed. The aberrations were never visible, but they were present all the same, sometimes detectable with the senses of smell or taste, but they usually seemed to accomplish their purpose.

The thought of this carelessness sent a feeling of revulsion through him. To attack the fundamentals of life, to disrupt the ancient processes of nature itself seemed like a recipe for disaster. But back then he never saw the danger, never realised how narrow the path they trod really was.

When the Self Immolating DNA string, or 'life's code of death', was discovered in a Cornwall testing site, the affected cases were immediately quarantined, but too late. Before long the site was a mass of rotting vegetation.

But incredibly the problem spread to the surrounding area, killing plants, livestock and in a few, very strange cases, people.

It swept through the Lizard, then the rest of Cornwall like wildfire, stopping for some reason at the river Tamar. Within months the county was a lifeless desert, as chemicals from the infected plants leached the soil of all life-supporting nutrients.

Now the only colour was grey, where there used to be green pastures. Scientists had said that nothing would grow there again, ever. For it was cursed, forsaken.

And so, in a way, was he, for the plants that had first shown signs of the rot, he reflected as he trudged back to the waiting Landrover that had brought him to this desolate spot, had been under his jurisdiction at the Lizard GM Testing Centre.

Will Robertson, aged 13,
Mullion School.

The West Briton 4 October 2070

Today is a sad day for Cornish farming, as the last farmer hangs up his wellies. Since the turn of the Millennium people have been flocking to Cornwall for the 'lovely scenery' and not just for holidays they wanted to stay.

More and more houses have been eating away at the countryside until today. The last farm was sold for land for yet another housing estate. The population explosion has completely destroyed the farming community of the whole of Cornwall. In 1999 there were hundreds of farms, but as the new Millennium dawned it brought with it a price crash on property in Cornwall. This prompted all those visitors who had been meaning to buy holiday homes in Cornwall to move. This placed a very high price on the land and the farmers could not afford to not sell.

As the last farmer retired we had an exclusive interview to see what he really thought of it all, 'I have been farming since I was a boy way back in 1999, as we saw in the new Millennium I knew there would be trouble. Nothing happened for a few years but then the prices on property crashed and people were flocking to buy the "bargain houses", since then it has just been a downward spiral. I've managed to hang on this long but now with no sons to pass the farm on to I have no option but to sell and let the land go to another budding entrepreneur who will no doubt make his millions with all the properties built on my land.' So that is the opinion of the last Cornish farmer ironically named Jack Farmer.

Cornwall is no longer self sufficient, it now relies on large chain stores such as Tesco to import it's food.

Alison Philpott,
aged 14,
Mullion School.

The Street where I live

The smell is what gets me every time; it's a cross between the countryside and early morning. It's hard to explain but the street where I live is two different worlds.

I must explain this first. My house is on Henver Road in St Columb Minor which is on the outskirts of Newquay, the front of my house edges on to the busy road into Newquay, we have a cafe and it's very busy all the time, but if you leave that behind and walk out to the back it's very different: the sea-side town merging into green fields and a farm, the land dips and steepens from which you can see a mass of pine trees. If you look to the right you can see for 20 miles over Cornwall to St Agnes Beacon, still further right and you see my school and the busy town of Newquay. Everyone along my side of the street has large gardens that merge into grain fields and grass, a few people have very old apple trees that grow giant autumn coloured apples.

My house was the first on our side of the street and the land was bought from the Duchy of Cornwall in the 1920s, originally only the little cottages were there across the street they have tiny windows and sunken roofs, that's all that was along our dirt track, the closest settlement was St Columb right down the valley.

It's great to live in my street. It's most like living somewhere deep in the countryside but always there is the hint of a bustling seaside town just half a mile down the road.

Lucy Alexander, aged 13,
Newquay Tretherras School.

the future economy of Cornwall

As the Millennium looms, Cornwall looks with anticipation to what it will bring for the economy. All walks of life will enter a new century as old meets young and as one we will pass through a new time.

The Eclipse left Cornwall in the dark for a few brief minutes, but as the sun re-emerged we were left to ponder when Cornwall itself and its people would benefit from the opportunities and lifestyles which blessed the rest of Britain.

Many locals feel that Cornish folk have been left in the dark for too long as the rest of the country competes with its own education, transport and leisure. Education in Cornwall exists little more than schools and libraries. We do not have the luxury of a university where local young adults can study in *their* county. As the youth of today begin to expect more from life, it is no wonder that they look further afield to study in their chosen career.

But then what jobs are there to choose from? As Cornwall exists mainly on the primary economy, young adults with degrees in medicine, law and business can find little hope of succeeding in prime jobs in this region. Those who do favour farming and mining must watch out as these resources come under threat from government policies and lack of funds.

Transport exists in order to keep Cornwall connected with the rest of the country but those of us within the area feel isolated between parts as bus routes and train journeys are far and few between. Lack of money prevents regular services similar to that of the major cities elsewhere. School buses are as full with children as other routes are empty.

Without tourism Cornwall would struggle to survive. The economy is kept alive by people who visit from cities with multiple transport links and countries with expansive education resources.

With miles of sandy beaches and natural outstanding beauty Cornwall is renowned for providing a welcome holiday break... but those of us who live in Cornwall want a break. We look forward to competing with the rest of the country. We want to educate our youngsters at our own university. We want them to leave home in order to set up their own homes in Cornwall as they succeed in local jobs.

As the Millennium draws closer we are optimistic that Cornwall will grow in strength, the shadow will pass and the light will fall over Cornwall; January 1st 2000.

Fiona Price,
aged 17,
Bodmin Community School.

My Field

Autumn time is best down here,
Everybody thinks it's the only year,
Tourists are gone and out of sight,
Even some birds take up flight.

There's rain, cold, and sometimes snow,
But the plants and crops continue to grow,
The farmers on tractors plough through their fields,
As all the Cornish still need their meals.

Potatoes, carrots, turnip and corn,
Gather the harvest before the new dawn,
Because when the fishermen return from the sea,
There'll be a great feast for me and thee.

So blow up the bridge and cut the wires,
Return once more to local suppliers,
We may be plump, we may talk funny,
But dreckly there will be lots of money.

The cows in the barn with snug warm straw,
The millennium is at the farmer's door,
A better life – not without a pasty,
Do anything else and things could turn nasty.

Give us a chance and we'll prove to you,
How very much we really can do.
It's all in the stars the future economy,
The eclipse showed me the wonders of astrology.

Jane Julyan, aged 15,
Truro School.

The Future...

A wise man once said, *'Cornishmen are fishermen and Cornish lads are miners too, but when the fish and tin are gone what are the Cornish lads to do?'* Sadly this proves true today.

In recent times the Cornish economy has felt decline, however with government assistance it is hoped things will be looking up.

The 'toe' of the British Isles is where our Celtic nation lies. The vast expanse of countryside, littered with ruins telling of a bygone industrial age. Mine houses stand silent reflecting this industry lost in time, for foreign imports have stolen local business.

Signs of an ancient civilisation are spread over the county, visitors admire stone crosses and monuments. Villages once thriving with business now depend on the annual influx of visitors.

Although our future looks somewhat bleak there is hope for the optimists amongst us. Cornwall boasts immense coastal beauty, tourism is a key player – development of green tourism draws travellers from near and far. Redevelopment of town centres increases economic potential. The internet truly is our 'highway to the world'; much business has already been brought here in this way. The prospect of a university promotes optimism in locals, opportunities are endless, and there is something for 'the Cornish lads to do'... Remain hopeful, and keep the Cornish spirit alive.

Laura Hancock, aged 17,
Bodmin Community College

The Future...

Cornwall's economical needs and identity have been denied for so many years that it has woken up at the end of the 20th Century as one of the poorest areas in the U.K., thus gaining, after a lengthy fight, the European Objective One status. What is to become of this injection of money to enable a stable and wealthy economy and a future for the Cornish?

As a young person my initial concern would be that education is taken as a priority subject for improvement. We are the only county without a University or research centre. Cornish people (considering the low average income) cannot afford to travel elsewhere for university training, which forces them into service jobs. Local employers wishing to recruit graduates have to bring people in from other parts of the U.K. This means that Cornish people have little chance of a decent wage instead having jobs providing inadequate family incomes causing the next generation to face the same problems. This cycle has left Cornwall's economy in a rut for which a university can provide the vital step-up to the stability of the economy.

The university will generate people with the qualifications and skills to form the basis of better quality employment. Cornwall has relied, for many years, on a primary economy which is declining rapidly, and a service economy paying very little. We have the opportunity to use Cornwall's resources to improve its main industries and widen the scope for new industries.

Tourism is one of Cornwall's booming industries, We should now focus on quality by utilising our culture and history, developing sporting assets and improving quality of towns to attract more affluent visitors from abroad.

Other industries can also be developed. We are surrounded on three sides by sea. This asset, which originally provided for the primary economy of fishing, can be utilised as a resource for an aquaculture industry. Part of this could be linked with the development of research into the uses of algae which can be exploited to bring a lot of money into Cornwall, proving greatly beneficial towards Cornwall's economy. If a couple of Cornwall's industries are the centre of vigorous plans for their growth, they can bring money back into Cornwall to fuel other growing industries allowing our economy to thrive.

Our poor infrastructure is hindering economic growth. Cornwall needs to have improved transport to attract new industries and to make the most of one of the best natural harbours on the south coast- Falmouth. The A30 needs to be dualled right into mid Cornwall. Improved air transport will be beneficial to international tourism and industry. These can all greatly boost Cornwall's economy. We can only hope that the right decisions are made and as we look into the next millennium we will see a future where Cornwall's economy will thrive and prosper.

Sterenn Le Nen Davey, aged 15,
Bodmin Community College

The Future...

The future economy of Cornwall could be a very boring subject to write about, but I have big plans for this fascinating county. Firstly I should look at the county's economy and then expand on it, the biggest income of money to the county comes from tourism, the county should take advantage of this by putting a big wall across the border between Devon and Cornwall, then you could charge an entrance fee, to visit this fascinating part of the world. When asked what has Cornwall got to offer the reply should be stunning scenery, amazing surf, a walker's paradise, and much more.

The county will soon be rivalling the south east, with Truro contesting for the capital instead of London. The fishing industry will take off and the income into the county will double, there will be high-tech boats taking to the water, catching more fish than anywhere else in the world. Over the next few years surfing as a sport will become internationally popular with world championship events being held throughout the year in Cornwall, overtaking football with big money sponsorship and support, bringing extreme wealth to Cornwall.

On the subject of watersports, yachting, water skiing, recreational fishing and power boat racing, will expand again providing lots of money for Cornwall. Someone in Cornwall will develop the county's capacity to provide power using ecologically friendly means, wind, waves and solar. There will be an abundance of this and we will be able to export it to the rest of the country and the world.

With all the profit an international sports stadium will be built, which will host the 2010 Olympic Games. Penzance Rugby side will have so much money that they can poach top players from Bath Rugby Club, and other top sides resulting in them winning the premier league. The same will happen to Truro Football club. Even though Cornwall will expand and become internationally the greatest county in the world, the area will not be ruined, with pollution or industrial areas, it WILL keep its beauty and peacefulness. The character of the county will stay the same.

All the big towns in Cornwall will include a well equipped sport and leisure centre encouraging youngsters to get off the streets and put all their energy into sport. In Truro there will be an international university catering for students from all around the world and providing an education better than anything Oxford and Cambridge could ever supply.

Christopher Price, aged 15, Truro School.

The Future...

Geographically, culturally and economically, Cornwall has long been considered a separate entity from the rest of the United Kingdom. Indeed, by many people Cornwall is thought to be almost a separate country. But why is Cornwall so different?

The answer lies in the traditions of Cornwall. Occupations have long centred around fishing, farming, mining and more recently tourism. However, with the advancements of modern technology and the fast approaching new millennium, the people of Cornwall are realising that something needs to change before Cornwall and its inhabitants are left behind.

One of the main problems for Cornwall is that it is the only county without a university. This means that for many jobs which require a university degree Cornish students have to leave their county or that people are employed from elsewhere which denies the Cornish employment.

A university would establish Cornwall. Whichever town would be chosen for the site, the town would build up around the student body. I feel Cornwall would be a strong attraction to university applicants.

Its rich heritage and beautiful scenery attract thousands of tourists each year and would interest students as well. By providing a university for Cornwall, the government will help bring us into the new millennium. The government could also help by improving transport around Cornwall. Many problems such as queues of traffic, pollution and fuel wastage stem from the transport problems of Cornwall. If this was improved Cornwall could be more efficient and it could help prevent rising pollution levels which are ruining our clear, clean air.

By improving Cornwall's transport and education, attraction to the area would precipitate to tourists. Cornwall already has a strong tourist industry and economical improvements would strengthen it further. However the Cornish people do not want to rely on tourists from other areas. We want to preserve our rich cultural back-ground and natural Celtic beauty whilst bringing Cornwall forward for the next millennium.

Amanda Henry,
aged 17,
Bodmin Community College.

Illustration by Darrien Gibson, aged 8; Daniel O'Hanlon, aged 9; Adam Yould, aged 3;
Gus O'Brien, aged 8; Amber Scott, aged 3; George Nixon, aged 3; and Oliver Nixon, aged 1.

The future of
Cornwall is

in your
hands...

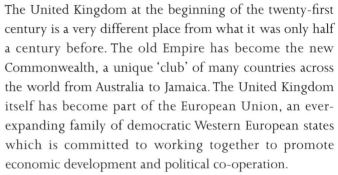

The United Kingdom at the beginning of the twenty-first century is a very different place from what it was only half a century before. The old Empire has become the new Commonwealth, a unique 'club' of many countries across the world from Australia to Jamaica. The United Kingdom itself has become part of the European Union, an ever-expanding family of democratic Western European states which is committed to working together to promote economic development and political co-operation.

As a result of widespread immigration after the Second World War, especially from Asian and Caribbean countries, the United Kingdom has an increasingly rich diversity of religions, languages, customs, foods, music, and dress, an important contribution to what has become known as our 'multicultural' society.

The way in which the United Kingdom is governed has also changed, with new Parliaments or Assemblies in Scotland, Wales and Northern Ireland. Everywhere, there is emphasis on giving power back to local communities, to letting regions decide many issues for themselves. There is also increased support for the Welsh, Scots Gaelic and Irish languages, part of the celebration of multiculturalism.

Cornwall, too, is a part of all this. Cornwall has its own special ties with the Commonwealth, the legacy of the nineteenth-century Great Emigration, and there are Cornish Associations throughout Australia, Canada, New Zealand and South Africa. There are also many Cornish Associations in the United States of America. Numerous people of Cornish descent from all over the world visit Cornwall frequently, an important boost to our tourist industry.

In the United Kingdom, the Cornish are recognised as one of the constituent British peoples. As the Prime Minister, Tony Blair, wrote in *The Times* on 12 February 2000: 'It is intrinsic in the nature of the Union [the UK] that we have multiple political allegiances; we can comfortably be Scottish and British or Cornish and British or Geordie and British or Pakistani and British'.

In the European Union, Cornwall has links with other regions, notably Brittany, another Celtic land with a language, Breton, very similar to Cornish. Many Cornish towns and villages are twinned with counterparts in Brittany. Cornwall County Council has a special twinning relationship with Finisterre, one of the Breton local government areas. There are close links too with Ireland, Scotland, Wales and the Isle of Man, placing Cornwall at the centre of the Celtic world.

Regions are set to become even more important within Europe, and Cornwall has been designated an economic region by the European Union. This has made Cornwall eligible for substantial financial aid from Europe, and for this reason it was given Objective One status, allowing Cornwall to draw large grants from the European Union to help fund economic development here.

For many years Cornwall has suffered from above average unemployment and below average earnings, and there have been other social problems such as poor health and poor housing. Cornwall's traditional industries have also been in decline.

However, Cornwall has successfully turned its hand to new industries, and today there are many thriving small businesses manufacturing 'hi-tech' products which are in demand the

world over. The *In Pursuit of Excellence* initiative, which has brought together businessmen and other community leaders from across Cornwall, has drawn attention to the wide range of new, successful companies producing goods for export. Objective One will help these companies to become even more successful, laying firm foundations for Cornwall's prosperity in the twenty-first century.

The widespread use of information technology means that geographical distance from business centres is no longer a disadvantage, and Cornish companies can compete success-fully with others elsewhere in the UK or Europe. But in other respects geography remains important. Cornwall's significant maritime location (with its stupendous natural harbour at Falmouth), means that it is exceptionally well placed to develop a maritime strategy for the twenty-first century, part of a wider strategy to identify our key strengths and to act upon them.

An attractive environment is another of Cornwall's strengths, as is the 'small scale' of so much of our social and economic activity. By and large we have avoided the worst of the socio-economic evils of the 'inner cities' up-country, and instead we have continued to value and to nurture our mixed town and country life, with its emphasis on community and co-operation. 'Small is Beautiful' is certainly true of Cornwall.

Cornwall's special identity is also a key strength, a major resource for the future. Pride of place has become increasingly important to regions throughout Europe. The confidence to get things done, to achieve, rests to a considerable degree on this 'pride of place'. So too does the ability to get noticed on the national and international stage. When Cornwall goes to Twickenham, its thousands of rugby supporters wearing black-and-gold and flourishing the flag of St Piran, the world sits up and takes notice.

Cornwall is also an unbeatable 'brand name', a by-word for distinctiveness but also for excellence. There is nothing quite like Cornish cream, or Cornish strawberries, or even Cornish potatoes, but in the realms of communications, micro-engineering, yacht construction, and many other areas of economic activity, 'Made in Cornwall' also means high quality and exceptional standards.

But to maintain, develop and market these qualities Cornwall needs its own institutions, and none more so than a University. Every year, thousands of students leave Cornwall to study 'up-country', and very few return – at least in the short term. A University for Cornwall would give many Cornish students the chance to learn locally. It might also stop the Cornish 'brain drain' and would be a powerful tool of economic development in its own right. Wherever there is a University there is also a vibrant economy, together with a broader cultural life and a wide range of supporting amenities. Students from elsewhere in the UK and from overseas would be attracted to a University here, helping to develop Cornwall as an international centre of excellence for academic study.

There is also much debate about what other kind of institutions Cornwall might need. For example, Cornwall today is part of the South West Regional Development Agency which extends as far as Gloucestershire and Wiltshire but many people have argued that we should have our own Cornish Development Agency.

The establishment of Assemblies for Scotland, Wales and Northern Ireland means that 'devolved' or regional governments may well be set up in other parts of the United Kingdom. Should this happen, then there is certain to be vigorous debate about what form of regional government might be best for Cornwall. Ought Cornwall to be part of a wider South West Region, or should Cornwall be a Region in its own right?

Whatever the outcome of such debates, there will be an increasing demand that Cornwall's children should have the right to live, learn, work and prosper here. This means building an economic and educational infrastructure to suit the needs of Cornwall.

And with economic security and educational opportunity will come cultural flowering, the celebration in word, picture, dance, play, and a host of other media, of Cornwall as a very special place. As multicultural Britain develops apace, and as regional diversity becomes ever more important within Europe, so Cornwall's identity will be an increasing source of pride, energy, enthusiasm and spiritual well-being on which to build a bright Cornish future.

A vision of Cornwall tomorrow is of a land of sustained and sustainable prosperity, of an enviable environment in which to live, learn, work and play, of a proud people who know that their identity is their greatest strength and who are never afraid to shout:

CORNWALL
FOR EVER!
KERNOW
BYS VYKEN!